TENDING THE FIRE

Creativity, Purpose, and the Unfolding Self

by
Enrique Martínez Celaya
and James Hollis

CHIRON PUBLICATIONS • ASHEVILLE, NORTH CAROLINA

www.ChironPublications.com

Interior and cover design by Danijela Mijailovic
Printed primarily in the United States of America.

Front cover painting, The Apple Tree, 2023, Oil and wax on canvas, 116 × 150 in. Courtesy of Studio Enrique Martínez Celaya. Private collection, Chicago

ISBN 978-1-68503-655-3 paperback
ISBN 978-1-68503-656-0 hardcover
ISBN 978-1-68503-657-7 electronic
ISBN 978-1-68503-658-4 limited edition paperback
ISBN 978-1-68503-659-1 limited edition hardcover

Library of Congress Cataloging-in-Publication Data Pending

For Mei-Lee Ney and Selma Holo
EMC

For Jill,
Taryn, Timothy, Jonah, Seah
JH

Preface

In the late spring of 2016, James Hollis was to speak in Los Angeles at the Jung Institute. As a result of reading *The Middle Passage*, Enrique Martínez Celaya asked to meet him for an hour or so. During that hour, despite our quite different backgrounds, careers, and professions, we found an instant compatibility. In time, we also learned that we had each come from working-class backgrounds, had each encountered—as life brings to all—some significant obstacles, had each altered our career trajectory, and had each undertaken substantial changes in our perspectives and in the conduct of daily life.

Through the years since, we have kept in contact only electronically as we live on opposite sides of the continent. Finally, in late autumn of 2024, Enrique shared an idea that had been germinating within him for some time—to engage more deliberately in a dialogue on questions we believed were implicit in our work, even more than in our intermittent conversations. We met on a video call and formulated questions that engaged each of us, then agreed to write a personal response to each and comment on each other's work.

Later, when we read each other's drafted responses, we dropped the mechanism of further commentary because we found that our separate histories had such an implicate similarity that further commentary was superfluous. Although we have different writing styles, approaches, and professions, at times we were surprised by coincidences in our lives and references in this book. The themes that emerged—creativity, meaning, selfhood, memory, loss, and integrity—were not new to us, but the process of returning to them in written dialogue gave them new urgency and form. Moreover, we each recognize that, for all the nuances of family and cultural milieu, we have been in the grip of an unfolding life—a life with many twists and turns, yet one guided by an inner thread. What carries us remains unknown, but something does, though it has been up to each of us to tend the fire that sparked in childhood and still burns intensely.

The form itself—alternating reflections without response or rebuttal—was meant to leave space for the reader, not to model agreement but to invite a parallel inner conversation.

Each reader may recall that as children, amid wonder, curiosity, and sometimes terror, we asked large questions. But, given the need to report to the world on a daily basis, those questions slowly faded and were replaced by adaptive strategies as each child sought to fit in, get needs met, and stay out of harm's way. These many years later, this life becomes so much habit, so much routinization, so many replicative outcomes. To return to these early questions is not a sentimental gesture but a difficult one—one that asks attention, honesty, and a willingness to be shaped again. Yet it is questions, not their putative answers, that make our lives interesting and developmental. It is our hope that by recovering some of those questions, now seen from the vantage point of decades of experience (one now sixty-one, one eighty-five), readers will be stirred, and perhaps challenged, to respond to them within the topography of their own quite different lives. As different as our paths are, we are all on the same journey. Asking questions that matter leads each of us to a frame of larger amplitude.

Welcome to these questions. They are at work already in your life. Bringing them to greater consciousness may well provide you with a larger frame, a larger journey, and a more interesting life.

Enrique Martínez Celaya — James Hollis
Los Angeles — Washington, D.C.

Be patient toward all that is unsolved in your heart and try to love the questions themselves, like locked rooms and like books that are now written in a very foreign tongue. Do not now seek the answers, which cannot be given you because you would not be able to live them. And the point is, to live everything. Live the questions now. Perhaps you will then gradually, without noticing it, live along some distant day into the answer.

Rainer Maria Rilke

The Questions

Life and Experience

Creativity and Engagement with the World

Life and Experience

1

What threads have you found in the course of your life that supported you, guided you, and corrected you?

If your Nerve, deny you—
Go above your Nerve.

Emily Dickinson

EMC: Certain questions do not belong to us alone. They arrive through us, carried by a current that has been moving long before we became aware of it. They often come unannounced, not so much seeking an answer as awakening something in us, and they return again and again in different forms across years and circumstances. The questions we have gathered here are of that kind. They ask to be lived with, each opening a territory for us to explore. Sometimes they demand effort and discipline, sometimes surrender, and almost always patience.

In my own life, the most important questions have arrived when I needed them, and I have felt as though it was not they who arrived but I, and that they had been waiting for me all along. They never appear too early or too late, though I don't always recognize their timing. Some of these questions have interrupted plans, altered directions, and kept me company when little else made sense. I trust them more than the answers I can offer in this book. Everything I write here is provisional, awaiting what unfolds in my life and in my intellectual and spiritual journey to show me what should be said.

This first question—*What threads have you found in the course of your life that supported you, guided you, corrected you?*—seems to ask not only about those threads but about the life they have held together. Therefore, before exploring these threads, I would like to consider the life such threads sustain, since we move through the years gathering practices, habits, and beliefs that appear helpful, often without knowing whether they carry us toward or away from ourselves. This question, like all of them in this book, is not about the past alone. It reaches into the present and asks who we are. If our threads sustain us within an inauthentic life, the guidance we receive, no matter how steady, reinforces a path that does not serve what is within us, allowing even the most deluded lives to persist. Time moves quickly when we live a life that isn't our own—there's always something to fix, something to acquire, someone to impress—and that constant motion disguises drift as purpose. When the rhythm of such a life becomes comfortable and familiar, it can take years to realize that steadiness itself may have been the disguise of self-deception.

Regardless of how solid it looks on the outside, this type of life is hollow, and something in the world or within us usually finds the void. In *Heart of Darkness*, Joseph Conrad writes:

> But the wilderness had found him out early, and had taken on him a terrible vengeance for the fantastic invasion. I think it had whispered to him things about himself which he did not

> know, things of which he had no conception till he took counsel with this great solitude—and the whisper had proved irresistibly fascinating. It echoed loudly within him because he was hollow at the core.

The whispers that find and uncover the hollowness of our life are not always dramatic or terrifying. More often, they are subtle—a sense of discontent, a growing distance from loved ones, an emptiness in our work, or the unfamiliarity of our own face in the mirror. Sometimes, they take the form of an interest we set aside that continues to call for our attention, or a question that refuses to fade: *What am I chasing?* or *Why does it never feel like enough?* Occasionally, they arrive as glimpses of the future, brought on by an unexpected event or accident.

One such moment came for Henri Matisse. He was studying law, the respectable career his father had envisioned for him, when, during his recovery from appendicitis, his mother gave him a box of crayons to pass the time. He would later describe the experience as a revelation: "From the moment I held the box of colors in my hands, I knew this was my life." These moments of confrontation can be relentless in what they reveal about ourselves and what we have left unlived. They force us to see the gap between the life we are living and the one we might have chosen had we been braver or more willing to listen to what had been stirring inside us. In

Matisse's case, the box of crayons was a summons, and he answered it.

Matisse hadn't progressed far in his law career, which likely made it easier for him to let it go. Often, what gives meaning and certainty to an inauthentic life is how invested we are in it, especially when that investment comes with success. Many of us interpret success as validation of our path, a view shaped and encouraged by religious and cultural myths. Across many traditions, success is presented as a reflection of concordance with a higher order, whether divine, moral, or natural. These messages resonate in a world eager for certainty, but they risk conflating external success with internal alignment. Success is easily mistaken for truth, yet accomplishments frequently come at the expense of ourselves. History is full of stories of people who achieved extraordinary feats but left legacies of anguish, doubt, and damage. Striving, especially in a culture that elevates self-improvement and productivity to an ethical mandate, can become its own form of enslavement. The relentless pursuit of success, framed as both validation and necessity, erodes the space needed for reflection and rest, reducing individuals to performers in a system that prizes output over meaning. True alignment, whether with purpose, morality, or a higher order, may require questioning success itself, disentangling it from striving, and recognizing that the life it builds can be hollow if driven by compulsion rather than choice.

To speak of threads is to speak of what holds us together, yet every thread binds as much as it supports.

The life they sustain depends on their nature and on our awareness of what they serve. A thread of devotion, for instance, can become a thread of servitude if it sustains an inauthentic aim; a thread of discipline can turn into rigidity if it no longer connects to meaning. This is why it matters, when we think or speak about our sustaining threads, to remain vigilant of the life they uphold. Every practice, belief, and attachment carries within it an assumption about what matters most. Without that vigilance, we risk mistaking endurance for faithfulness, or familiarity for truth, and the very threads that once steadied us can begin to constrain us.

In my case, questioning success and seeking a deeper alignment with my own convictions rather than inherited expectations became a turning point. By my mid-twenties, I had achieved many of my family's career dreams and my own. With a recurring sense that my worth depended on accomplishment, I accumulated awards and prizes throughout high school and, as an undergraduate at an Ivy League school, worked at a nuclear accelerator—research I continued at a national lab over the summers while pursuing a graduate degree in physics. All of that seemed like confirmation of proper alignment and a promising future, and that, along with my gained facility in living in a new country with a new language, gave me a new sense of freedom.

Freedom sometimes appears in some aspects of what we do and who we are, while others remain enslaved to our notions of success, desire, fear, obligations, trauma, need. I began to sense this division in myself, though

I could not yet face it. Still, despite a growing unease, and clear signs that I didn't fit the mold I had shaped for myself, I held to the belief that the success I had attained meant I was where I needed to be.

But that conviction began to fray three years into my doctorate. Without fully understanding what I was doing, and to the dismay of my family, friends, and faculty advisors, I put my studies in physics on hold to paint, taking a job at a laser company in Palo Alto to cover my rent and materials. That step took courage, but also preserved a connection to my old life and its standards of success. Until one day, weary of the in-between life of scientist by day and artist by night, I found myself driving toward Pigeon Point, a lighthouse on a rugged cliff overlooking the Pacific—the remotest place I could reach by car on short notice.

What happened there was a confrontation with the life I had built and the identity I had shaped. I had to face the possibility that both were keeping me from the responsibility and freedom of shaping a life truer to who I was and to the world as it was, rather than to how I had been conditioned to see it. Until then, with the support and guidance of many threads, I had moved toward something certain without asking seriously enough whether that certainty aligned with what felt true to me. This critical, if elusive, dynamic between sustenance and direction is why I began my answer to the question of the threads that supported, guided, or corrected me by first considering what kind of life they sustain. Looking back, I see that as I paced that rocky shore what I was struggling toward was not just a shift in profession but a different way of being. Whether I realized it or not, the more alignment there was between my heart and my actions, the more I could rely on the internal forces, instincts, and values that had sustained me before, now engaged authentically with the world and with myself.

One thread that proved especially useful during that period of discovery and reinvention was my resistance to accepted wisdom, or even to my own opinions, unless they felt right. This resistance wasn't always obvious. Sometimes it remained internal, vague, no more than an unarticulated doubt, taking years to surface. But ultimately, it was this indispensable thread that guided and corrected me during those days at the lighthouse. It operated mostly unconsciously until it broke through when I was ready to pay attention. It had been there before the lighthouse, it was there during those five days, and it has remained with me ever since.

As an artist, the willingness to challenge received ideas and certainties is essential, and while it carries risks, I was never afraid of them. Art has nurtured this confidence while keeping it from hardening into hubris. In different but connected ways, art and the world have revealed the beauty at the heart of things, the interplay of tenderness and destruction, and the sustaining tension between transience and permanence. In doing so, they have shown me that questioning is not mere defiance, not a restless urge to reinvent the wheel or reject meaning, but a pursuit of something that endures both time and scrutiny.

This morning, as I sit at my kitchen table, I am reminded how those revelations of art and the world appear not only in reflection but in the very universe of which I am a part. I watch the breeze move through the wispy leaves of the Chinese elm outside my window while the early sunlight begins to lift the sky above the trees. Some of that light falls across the walnut grain of the table before me, touching the dying lilies in the vase where I placed them four days ago. It is too much beauty and truth to hold all at once, but what I manage to take in is enough to illuminate my understanding of what happened yesterday and who I am today, and when I get to the studio later, it will serve as both a catalyst for the work and a point of reference. Moments like this make clear why art has never felt like something I do, but something that has worked on me, shaping how I see and who I am.

My artistic practice has been one of my strongest, most trusted supports and guides. It has offered me a mirror when I needed it—and, most critically, when I didn't want it—and it has opened a window when my thoughts and vision needed greater awareness of the world and others. When I could no longer follow the God of my childhood, art created a different theology for me, and it has remained a faithful and honest companion.

Another thread that revealed itself at the lighthouse, and which I rely on increasingly now, was the skill of making room for parts of myself that I didn't fully understand and other parts that I didn't like, but knew I couldn't deny if I hoped to live honestly. I mentioned earlier the importance of living an authentic life, and perhaps few attitudes are more conducive to it than making room for those aspects of ourselves that are difficult to reconcile with who we think we are or tell ourselves we are. When I was a physicist, my deep interest in unresolved emotions and in activities pursued for their own sake felt like a distraction and proof that my Caribbean mind was ill-suited to the uncluttered mental clarity the field seemed to demand. Yet it was the acknowledgment and incorporation of these seemingly feral interests into my life and work that later rescued my artistic practice from the classicism I had imitated as an apprentice and allowed me to recognize my own vision.

Although I didn't consciously recognize my resilience, during those days at Pigeon Point, some part of me knew I could endure the break from physics and devote myself to art, a conviction shaped partly by my family and partly by the hard realities of exile. My parents could have justifiably given up many times, yet they kept going despite having no safety nets, no family nearby, and little assurance that the future would be kind. There have been moments when life, as Robert Frost says, has felt too much like a pathless wood, but burns and lashes of twigs across my eyes have clarified what truly matters. In this way, resilience has tempered my inclination toward an inauthentic life and tested the integrity of my resolve.

Another important thread in my life has been the instinct to seek out people and mentors who could help me grow, teach me what I needed to learn, and guide me. In my teens, to name just one period, there was Bart Mayol, with whom I apprenticed; José Manuel Alonso, my high school principal, who helped open my eyes to the world and to myself; and my high school teachers, Silgia Navarro and Juan Antonio Ramos, who revealed to me the power of art and literature. But not all my guides are people I have met. Many of the works, ideas, and lives I admire I have only known through books.

Of the several other threads I could name, let me mention just one more: the willingness to accept being perceived as difficult. My commitment to the values, attitudes, and standards in art and life that I consider worthwhile has sometimes set me at odds with other people's expectations. It took me a long time to accept this judgment without feeling the need to correct it, but that acceptance has been essential to coming to terms with myself and the integrity of the life I want to live. I don't believe that close-mindedness is a productive approach to life, so I make efforts to ensure that my sense of what is right is not rooted in ego, vanity, or pride. And when I am wrong, I try to recognize it, though more often than I'd like, it happens begrudgingly. Still, there's no denying that being thought of as difficult is uncomfortable. At times, I want to give in, and when little is at stake, I often do. But when I sense that what is being asked of me is a compromise of values or ideas I respect, I accept being perceived as difficult. I'm not sure how much choice I've had in this stance, but the willingness to bear that judgment has been a sustaining force in my life. All too frequently, we compromise our beliefs, our humanity, and our compassion in order to get along, be liked, or profit. Our cynical age has convinced many that these diminished expectations and the vague stance they create are signs of progress, sophistication, or liberation. I think it is quite the opposite. Liberation, sophistication, and progress rely on pursuing truth and remaining firm in that pursuit, even when it seems unreasonable or unpopular.

The threads that sustain a life do not spare us from isolation, doubt, failure, or loneliness, nor do they eliminate the risk of becoming lost or living an inauthentic life. What they offer is a way of providing support when we think there's none, and means of orienting ourselves and returning to what matters when we drift. Some of these threads are inherited, woven into us by the people and circumstances that shaped us. Others are found along the way, in the work we do, in the questions we ask, and, as I have found more and more, in the silences where a deeper awareness makes itself known. I have relied on my threads during the easy times, and much more when things have been difficult.

Earlier, I spoke of the struggle in my mid-twenties to accept the exhortation to live a more authentic life. The years since have only made clearer how easily one can remain stuck in what works, or be pulled into directions that seem necessary or inevitable but that lead away from oneself and the present. One challenge is not just recognizing the threads that sustain us, but trusting them. The harder challenge, perhaps, is letting them guide us without becoming rigid, allowing them to correct us and put us at risk without turning them into a crutch for certainty.

JH: We know that approximately every seven years, every cell in our body has died and been replaced by another, all thirty-seven trillion of them, although after the late twenties at a slowing rate. We also know that a significant percentage of household dust is discarded human skin cells. So, if you look under there, someone is coming or going, and since it is your bed, it is probably you.

Certainly nature is not invested in our perpetuation. It seems rather devoted to rapid recycling. We think of aging, dissolution, and death as the great antagonist, the Other who threatens us, forgetting all the while that death is our daily companion, not only in our existentially precarious perch above an abyss of annihilation, but in the sundry deaths of daily concourse. Our cells are dying; our understandings are dying; even memory dies if we live long enough, but something abides, and something is served by this dying, even though the ego is not thrilled by this reminder of its constraints.

So what keeps constancy in all that flux? The pre-Socratic Greek philosopher Heraclitus said "all is fire," that is, energy flickering, consuming, transforming, all the time. Nor, he added, may we step twice into the same stream for the second time the stream has flowed onward, and so have we. So, what keeps constancy, then? Plato asked for the person who could show him the One among the many and he would embrace that person to his heart's core. Goethe adopted as his motto, "*Was dauert im Wechseln*, What abides amid change?" And Gerard Manley Hopkins in his poem "That Nature is a Heraclitean Fire and of the Comfort of the Resurrection," answers the paradox of "Man, how fast his firedint, his mark on mind, is gone!" with his faith in the resurrection as the abiding element. And in the poem "Lament," Rilke balances his knowledge of the stars burning out with his intuition about which one, perhaps only one, that "at the end of its long beam in the sky still stands like a white city." What a lovely image, assuaging for the moment the existential Angst rising from our question of continuity amid change. As a child, I learned from my third grade teacher that it took roughly eight minutes for the light to arrive from our sun. I immediately thought to myself: if the sun already clicked off, we just do not know it yet. The light is still traveling our way. But, then, perhaps it didn't… . I recall that I was more curious about that event than contemplating what the consequences of all that might portend.

As we all know, the only constant is change. We may even use this truism as a lens through which to see the culture wars and internal conflicts that consume so much of modern cultures, including the United States. While there are many, many factors that feed those anxieties, I surmise that the rapidity of change is chief catalyst for cultural anxieties. Yes, vast industries die, move off shore, dislocating the economic situation of millions. Climate change is hard upon us and an ongoing existential threat. But most of all is the loss of "fixities." "Fixities" is my coinage to refer to what folks historically believed was "fixed" in nature, or by divine fiat.

My parents, along with their coevals, believed that there were clear and normative definitions of what it meant to be a man or a woman. They believed that there were fixed moral systems, fixed sexual identity and sexual practices, certainties such as "that old time religion," and that institutions like government, universities, medicine, and other pillars of democratic systems were fixed, inviolable, and perpetuating. Until they were not.

Somewhere, after WWII, those "fixities" were deconstructed. Some of us learned that all those categories were human constructs, and what humans have made, can be deconstructed just as well. Some of us learned not to depend on those outer entities, or presume their perpetual presence, and others experienced anxiety to their cores and have made every effort from fundamentalism in religion to regressive governments to reconstitute the illusion of the old fixities. (For example, the two sectors of the "religious" spectrum to grow since WWII are fundamentalism, and its opposite: thirty percent of the American public who endorse no institutional creed nor believe in a divine being.) While there are moments of push and pull, the ineluctable flow of change is irresistible.

This decline of an older, institutionalized vision is common to the history of humankind. Gods die, despite their immortal claims. The catalogues of deities long past is as long as human history. When, for example, a little over two millennia ago a terrible rumor swept the

Mediterranean cultures that the god Pan had died, it produced "panic." Panic occurs when we find ourselves suddenly in new terrain where the old map is no long applicable. Gods die when the image can no longer contain the once vital energy, no longer move humans in the old earth-shaking way. What is dead is not the energy that goes elsewhere to incarnate in some new form, but the old image's capacity to hold it, perhaps let it shine through in luminous revelation. These historic or personal moments often lead one to seek either to reconstitute the old order ("make our God great again"), or seek a life of numbing or distraction that pretty much sums up the flavor of modern Western culture.

Where does one turn when the outer proves less and less reliable? Well… for one thing, to various forms of narcosis, that is, numbing through busyness, consumerism, substances of various kinds, but most of all distraction. As far back as the seventeenth century Blaise Pascal noted the need for *divertissement* lest even royalty, with all its privileges, grow terrified to confront the abyss of the self. As more and more moderns intuit the abyss which lies beneath them, the more these diversions grow compelling and addictive. And as we know, all addictions are reflexive anxiety management systems. Offering a moment's distraction or respite, they must be repeated as the great unknown begins to slosh around our feet, lap about our ankles. It is clear that the future belongs to those who are flexible, those who can learn and grow into the new message the Other has brought us. But there is always a conservative part of us that wants predictability, certainty, and of course control, even as it is forever challenged by the otherness of the Other that courses on in its unstoppable fashion.

One never knows what is going to bring one into proximity with the mystery, with the possible terrors of the unknown. Two days ago, a large buck with antlers crashed into our car. For a micro-moment he and I faced each other through the windshield. It was, among other things, a reminder of the utter unpredictability of life, the utter absurdity of things. It has left me wondering what its meaning might be for me. Or is there no meaning to be found, other than that one saw so often in the ancient classical texts and scriptures: "Never Presume." How far away is that aneurism, that heart attack, that assault on the expectations which we carry into each day?

In my last book, *Living with Borrowed Dust*, I concluded a chapter on trauma with these prose words which a friend, having passed through a medical ordeal of his own, quoted back to me, although he arranged it on the page as if it were a poem:

> *We Need to Remember*
> that not everything gets healed,
> that justice is not always the outcome,
> and that the work of healing may take a lifetime.
>
> This means we may have to live
> with matters unresolved,
> with injustice reverberating in our splintered bones,

and the discrepancies between
what we wish for our lives and
what is achievable is often very great indeed.

Accordingly, we all have to live with loss
and treasure what we can wrest from it.

We have to live with disappointment
and savor how blessed we are.

We have to live with unachievable desires
and be grateful for how they helped us
move more fully into life and its struggles.

I believe those words, and would not have written them in their prose version if I did not, but talk is cheap. Each new encounter with the mysterious other in life is a challenge both to hold to something constant within us, and to learn what the encounter has to teach us.

One of the hardest things I ever learned, and need to keep learning anew, is the power of the other within each of us. In my chosen field of depth psychology, both a discipline and a way of seeing that seeks to engage with the unknown, to dialogue with the unconscious, we view psychopathology somewhat differently than other healing modalities. It is natural for the ego-driven world, a world that offers much richness, to wish to rid itself of suffering as soon as possible, but from an analytic perspective we rather ask these heuristic questions: *why has this come to me, what is its summons, how am I to reframe my understanding of self and world as a result?* These questions are not easy, obviously, but they do lead us to a developmental dialogue with that other over which we may have no outer powers of resolution.

Analytic work is very humbling, for it repeatedly teaches us the impossibility of ego-sovereignty over our world. But, rather, the ongoing project is to bring the ego into a more harmonious relationship with the other energies of the psyche, lest we remain at odds with ourselves and further our uncivil war within. The psyche, like other elements of nature, is a constantly shifting cluster, so this work is life-long. One does not get "analyzed," as some have fancied, but one's aroused awareness is summoned to an on-going state of vigilant attendance upon the passage of things.

For example, at mid-life, I had achieved virtually all of my goals: a loving family, career success, and worthy professional challenges. And then a depression took over in my thirties. At that time, I naturally sought surcease of suffering as soon as possible. I went to a psychiatrist who gave me medications that seemed to dull me not move me in any direction. Finally, and to his credit, he referred me to the only Jungian analyst then residing between New York and Washington. Thus, the adventure began. Though I did not know it at the time, I was beginning the second half of the journey, a journey that continues to this minute.

Given that the psyche is itself evolving, as well as responding to new environmental changes, one never has certainty although the ego consciousness can easily delude us into thinking we know enough to know enough. What the ego needs to learn, and respect, is that *there is an Other within each of us that knows us better than we know ourselves, is seeking its expression in the world through us, and is constantly embodying messages that are corrections of course, whether within the body, the mind, or in the phantoms of the night that haunt us.* Thus, to the dismay of the ego consciousness, psychopathology is not something to be suppressed but rather to be queried to see *why it has come, what it is asking of us, and how are we to conduct our journey hereafter.*

Little did I know then, decades ago, that the depression was informing me that I had some business to address other than that which had occupied my conscious life until then. I am both haunted by, and challenged by, the question C. G. Jung asked when he queried what supports us when nothing supports us. Only after a long while, did I come to realize that that "support" often arrived as a set of symptoms not to be conquered but with which to dialogue. And perhaps to grow. Whuddathunk such a thing?

When in his last years he came to sum up his life with his memoirist Aniela Jaffe, Carl Jung resisted pronouncing any grave truths. In fact, in the concluding chapters of *Memories, Dreams, Reflections*, his account is touchingly modest and unadorned: "I cannot form any final judgement because the phenomenon of life and the phenomenon of man are too vast.... I only know that I was born and exist, and it seems to me that I have been carried along. I exist on the foundation of something I do not know. In spite of all uncertainties, I feel a solidity underlying all existence and a continuity in my mode of being." I would second those conclusions. The more we know, the more we know we know not. And yet, that same child we were, with all its thousand outer changes, is still who we are today—full of wonder, existential angst, and an insatiable curiosity. So the underlying continuity is palpable. But what is the underlying support that we intuit? We shall leave that question for another section of this book.

2

How do you make important decisions? With examples.

this was the question
that destroyed Agamemnon, there on the beach,
the Greek ships at the ready, the sea
invisible beyond the serene harbor, the future
lethal, unstable: he was a fool, thinking
it could be controlled. He should have said
I have nothing, I am at your mercy.

Louise Glück

JH: The word "decide" means to cut through with a knife, perhaps to cut off the contretemps with a conclusive action. It means, at times, to cut through the resistance, whether outer or inner. Sometimes one decides by granting one's group, or partner, or one's cultural conditioning to have final say in our decisions. Sometimes one decides impulsively, and may thereafter regret the quick decision. Sometimes we decide on the spot and it proves to have enduring legitimacy. For example, decades ago, in a foreign country, my wife and I, not looking to start a relationship, went to dinner for the sake of companionship and conversation in English for a change. Both of us decided that night, not that we would marry each other, but that in each other the kind of person we might want to marry was present. These many moons later, we are still exploring that proposition, and now in its fifth decade, have some suspicions this relationship might work out.

While it may always be rational, prudent, and practical to solicit the opinion of others in making important decisions, sometimes only a vote of one person, ours, is needed. For who really can see into the soul of another and know what is right for them? I recall Jung's colleague, Marie-Louise von Franz, saying that as an analyst she never pretended to know what is right for another person. However, she believed, and I concur, that something inside of each of us knows what is right for us and she added that she tried to pay attention to that discovery process with such patience and fidelity that in time that person would know what is right for them. Having perhaps achieved a measure of clarity, if not certainty, the immediate task is then to assemble the courage and the consistency to live their way into their unique embodiment of that decision.

All of us have some degree of "co-dependence" in our operative systems. We were, after all, socialized to fit in, perhaps punished in some way when we did not, and rewarded by being accommodating. I have sometimes called myself a "recovering nice person." The opposite of a reflexively co-dependent person is not a "bad" person, but an authentic person. While there is no Twelve Step group for such a species as recovering "nice" persons, co-dependence can be a severe disorder. At worst, such a person never gets to live his or her own journey for the will or expectations of the Other is forever paramount in the calculus of decision-making.

How many times does a person carry a life-long depression, while maintaining a happy front, or self-medicating the deep wound to the soul within, because they do not have "permission" to be who they are, desire what they desire, and go fight for what they wish in their lives? Co-dependence is a message over-learned in childhood where our tiny estates, our lack of role models, and our general powerlessness communicates to us that "the Other has the power, you do not, and satisfying their wishes will prove advantageous or perhaps necessary for you." It a legacy of the asymmetrical powers between the child and the adult, or in later years the adult and the community. If it were not for the autonomous recrudescence of symptoms, we would scarcely examine this discrepancy even if something gnaws within for all the days leading up to the present.

During my childhood, we would reach the resolution of questions with a simple system. "Eeeny, meeny, miney mo / Catch a tiger by the toe. / If he hollers make him pay / Fifty dollars every day." But then, there was a variation to this sage advice. If the person caught in the dilemma did not like the outcome, he might add, "My Mother told me to choose this best one!" It just so happens the odd number of syllables for the addendum reversed the choice seemingly just made by the august god of chance. It did not take this child long to tumble to the fact that the addition of the appendix, and sometime an appendix to the appendix, led to the reversal of outcomes, thus revealing what the person covertly wished in the first place.

A variant of this dilemma appeared in Aristophanes play *The Frogs* two and a half millennia ago. Heracles is sent into the underworld to bargain with the gods of the lower realms for the return of one of their great playwrights for, as stated in the book of Proverbs, "without vision the people perish." As it is a comic slant on a perduring dilemma, the protagonist goes though repeated tests to determine the greater playwright. Finally, at a loggerheads within, Heracles triggers the *deus ex machina*, and Athena is lowered to the stage to make a decisive resolution. But what she says to Heracles is as stunningly simple as that playground game: "choose that one in whom thy heart delights." That is to say, you respect them all, but you love one of them. Go with that.

Would that one's struggles with co-dependence could be resolved so simply and directly. Real life decisions are those in which no matter what one does, there is a significant cost to self and others. Pseudo-issues have black and white solutions. Real dilemmas place one on the rack. A narcissist, or a person owned by a complex, will make an impulsive or a self-serving resolution, but a deeply ethical person will suffer the dilemma to the core. Real issues will cost something important either way.

Both Jung, von Franz, and other Jungians have written about this sort of dilemma and have recommended the holding of the tension of opposites as long as one can until the third appears. Often the role of the therapist is to help that person find the patience and the courage to hold that tension when every fiber in one's being wishes immediate resolution. But what is that third? Generically, when one is up against a personal dilemma, the third is neither this one nor that one, but what that particular decision calls for in personal growth, or what larger vision of one's journey is seeking to come into play. For example, a common therapeutic dilemma: should person X stay in their marriage or not? Appealing to external authorities produces a response that maintains the status quo at the cost of something dear within that person. Or, jumping ship may suggest a narcissistic expression of self-interest that seemingly facilitates resolution but in fact is a regression. Accordingly, the way I put it to clients is, speaking of one choice or another, "what does this choice serve inside of you?" That is not a simple question and may have to be held as long as possible until its recondite answer emerges. In one case, one is acting on impulse; on the other hand, the person is simply taking an easy way out, a flight from conflict and confrontation. What to do, then?

If we can see our way through to the deeper psychospiritual values in play, and find the courage to live them, then we will grow into the next stage of our journey. It we cannot, then the noisiest complex of the hour has prevailed.

In my personal life, I can assure the reader that, historically, the largest number of my early life choices probably rose out of an archaic co-dependence, and/or fear of the judgement of others. We are all, of course, recovering children, so why would these early dangers and coping skills not hang around for a lifetime? My lack of permission to express myself emotionally was reinforced many times in childhood after being punished for expressing myself in normal instinctual ways. For example, when once I was angry and expressing my protest at the abuse of another child, I had a garden hose turned full blast upon me and told that would cool me down. I felt doubly abused then, and even more, forbidden to feel what I was feeling. Or when, as a seventeen year old I asked to borrow the family car to take a classmate on my first date, I was given the silent treatment for days. Message reinforced, many times in many different ways.

Rising out of such a milieu, how could one not doubt the reality of one's feelings and desires? How could one not think the inner world a source of discord and peril? How could one in mid-life not have a depression as one's psyche rebels at one's unwitting collusion in emotional oppression? To this hour, the historically generated tendency to shut down the inner life is reflexively present. It is the first response. What was once protective is now, of course, constrictive. It all had to get bad enough to produce a serious depression and to wind up leading me all the way to Zürich to suffer the *catabasis*, the descent into the underworld. Having lost my way at mid-life I had entered the proverbial dark wood of Dante's paradigmatic catabasis. Emerging from that dark wood took years, and is a continuing project. This is why Jung said of our core wounds, we do not "solve" them, but we can outgrow them.

It took me a long time to recognize that something within me really knew what was right for me. So incursive had been the boundary violations of childhood that I invested too much in the ego's operational plans. I had achieved all my plans by the time I was twenty-seven. And I kept achieving them for some years to come. Before the near-lethal depression arrived, I had spent so much effort in trying to please people, to do the "right thing," that I had become a stranger to myself. While there was nothing outwardly "wrong" with those outer choices and agendas, the question "what is this really in service to" had not occurred to me. Until it did.

There are moments in one's life when one "sees." Mid-life Gautama "saw," and that is how he became the Buddha, a Sanskrit word that derives from the verb "to see." Occasionally, one sees. I attribute my "seeing" less from what I read, though that was rich and wonderful, but more from those dark hours when I was forced to my knees and desolate. In one memorable series of dreams I was in a prison cell. (Imagine that.) In the final scene I realized a person I knew in real life had the key to let me out. I so requested and was rebuffed. As I reflected on the dream its obvious intent was to tell me I was asking something of another that I needed to ask of myself. That day, as I walked out of analysis, the analytic work moved from a commitment of the mind to a felt experience of the heart. I knew from that hour, and others like it, that something inside of me knew what was right for me and that I had to not only access that perspective ("choose that in which thy heart delights") but find the courage to live it into the world.

Many such experiences have led me into a progressive, and on-going, recovery of personal authority, a project I consider the chief task of the second half of life. The first half of life is often a gigantic, well-intentioned mistake whereby we are either serving what is being expected of us from our environment or running from it. The second half is instead characterized by, challenged by, the task of acquiring sufficient ego-strength, enough life experience upon which to reflect, and perhaps enough pain to be obliged to undertake the project of revisioning one's life. Only then can one begin to make the acquaintance of the little people down in the solar plexus, or wherever they reside. (I call the process of sorting and sifting which goes on inside of each of us, "The Little People," whom I presume reside in the solar plexus and work on these matters and sooner or later get back to us in their own good time, not our impatient time).

Today I know, and frequently have to wait upon, the report of the little people. They always get back to me, but the old me still wishes they would tell me the most pain-free, direct route to the future, or perhaps the scenic route, not the one that costs so much struggle. But in the end, I know they are right, and my path forward was laid out not by childhood, nor by the years of well-intentioned learning, but by the gods whose energies course within, and whom we must ultimately serve with humility. (When I speak of "the gods," it is not a theological or metaphysical locution; rather I mean the personified form of the archetypal energies that course through history, our bodies, and the dreams we dream tonight.) Perhaps we can finally understand the place and mission of those little people. They are the servants of the gods, the faithful instruments of their transcendent will for us. In the end, are we not all called to confess along with Agamemnon, "I have nothing, I am at your mercy." And out of that we have to make our life as best we can.

EMC: Most decisions worth making are not the result of clear logic or perfect timing but arise from the tension between knowledge and uncertainty. We are often told that decisive people know exactly what they want, that success belongs to those who follow one path without hesitation. Yet most significant decisions resist that simplicity. They unfold less like orders of will and more like movements of attention, responsive, adaptive, sometimes hesitant. We like to think that good decisions come from analysis or experience, yet most of what guides us happens below our cognition—accumulated intuitions, half-remembered lessons, the residue of past mistakes. By the time we face a choice, much of the decision has already been taking shape in us, through the slow accumulation of what we've lived and learned. Every decision that matters involves a balance between resolve and receptivity, between the desire to act and the willingness to listen to what the world, and something within us, might be saying. Sometimes what allows a decision to emerge is not greater certainty, but the quieting of what we think we already know. And how we decide—what we trust, what we resist—often reveals more about who we are than the outcomes of those decisions.

The process of painting can be understood as a long sequence of decisions, accompanied by reversals and failures that lead to further decisions. Yet before the first mark is made, we come to our work with a preexisting sense of what painting is, who we are, and what we hope to achieve. In this way, a painting begins years before the painter stands before the canvas. Prior knowledge, along with the assumptions, ambitions, and deliberations that shape it, can be both an asset and a barrier: useful for the experience it carries, but often an obstacle to engaging the work in the present. When painters recognize this, they try to strip away these preconceptions so they can meet the moment directly, even if doing so means surrendering aspects they once considered essential to their identity. This pursuit of freshness may be the artist's best, if not only, hope of creating something authentic.

By "surrendering aspects they once considered essential to their identity," I mean it in a narrow sense. As with our understanding of life, artists' understanding of art is ingrained in their intuitions, influences, values, and conceptual frameworks. So even a radical surrender amounts to a small shift—a nudge out of their own way. Yet, as small as that nudge might seem, it can resonate profoundly.

Despite its value, nudging ourselves out of the way, even modestly, proves difficult in practice. One of the most common issues I observe when talking to students or artists trying to improve their work is how protective they are of *what they do* and *who they are*, often conflated into the limiting idea of *their style*. Like many of us, they are consumed by doubts about their skills, interests, knowledge, background, or resilience. Fearing these doubts, they build walls around the certainties they've managed to gather, trying to shield them from being contaminated by doubts. Often unconsciously, they search for proven strategies to escape the discomfort of living with doubts about their work and themselves. Inevitably, their work suffers, not because doubt undermines it, but because their fear of doubt hardens their practice into something predictable. This fear, combined with the importance placed on novelty, creates late modernity's version of the Cowardly Lion: brash and fearless in appearance, but with a frightened heart.

It's easy to see why artists long to make decisions about their work without the unease that doubt brings. As artists, we've already taken a risk: the chances of even modest success are slim, there is no clear career path, society places little value on art, and support from one's community is often scarce. That's a lot of uncertainty before even facing a blank canvas, trying to hold on to the hope of significance while fearing failure. It's no surprise, then, that we sometimes make decisions strategically, cautiously, only to find that in shutting out doubt, we invite the very failure we were trying to avoid.

And this is not just the case for artists. Anyone attempting something without guaranteed outcomes must face doubt. This isn't a flaw that arises in certain vocations or temperaments, but part of the structure of life itself. We live without assurances, making many of our decisions in the dark, always lacking important information, yet hoping our efforts will lead to something lasting or true. Doubt arises not because we've lost our way, but because we are trying to find meaning in a world that is exuberant, mysterious, often confusing, and that offers no fixed answers.

To create, to care, and to believe are all acts of vulnerability exposed to uncertainty. The instinct to protect what we know, to cling to what feels stable, is one of the ways we try to manage that vulnerability. Whether in work, relationships, or personal convictions, we often retreat into certainty or dogma not because it is true, but because it is familiar. When we do, we risk becoming rigid and disconnected from the deeper sources of insight and vitality. Doubt, unwelcome as it often is, may be what keeps us honest and open.

I too treated doubt as an obstacle to overcome or avoid. As a child and young adult, I believed doubt was a sign of weakness. I was drawn to science partly because it seemed to promise methods to arrive at truth without ambiguity. Doubt felt like a crack in the system, or worse, in myself. And in many areas of life, I found that I was stubbornly holding on to positions and opinions, not because I believed the claims were necessarily right, but because conviction, even when grounded in error, provided reassurance. In a life impacted by exile and poverty, where many things felt unstable or subject to change, certainty—even false certainty—offered a rare anchor to hold on to. Even in my early teens, when I began to paint and draw, I carried this discomfort with me, trying to make decisions cleanly and decisively.

The first time I realized that doubt was worth considering came during a lucky encounter when I was fourteen. One afternoon, feeling anxious about a decision I needed to make, I shared my struggle with my school principal. We had gotten to know each other, and I trusted him—he would eventually become one of the most influential mentors in my life. We sat together on one of the concrete benches in the schoolyard, as we often did once or twice a week, and he listened patiently as I tried to make sense of my hesitation. "I wish I didn't have doubts," I finally said, frustrated with myself.

He looked at me for a moment, then said gently, "If you had no doubts, it wouldn't be a decision. Making a decision means choosing in the presence of doubt. Without doubt, there's nothing to decide."

What he said struck me as true right away. I looked at him and nodded. My decision wasn't any clearer, but some of the frustration was gone. That was the first time I'd considered that doubts and decisions are inseparable, but it would take me many more years to appreciate the value of doubts, and even longer to treasure them.

The main reason I found decisions about my life so puzzling was that I could usually see different paths, each containing a measure of truth. This coexistence of possibilities fascinated me in the context of quantum mechanics, one of my passions at the time, but it was deeply unsettling in human affairs, where I longed for certainty. Naively, I believed that if I thought hard enough, every situation had a right answer, a clear path to follow. And I wasn't only wrestling with my own multiplicity of opinions. Everywhere I turned, people seemed eager to tell me what I should do. My parents, friends, teachers, priests, television programs, my mother's friends chatting over coffee on Sundays, politicians, coaches, even the artist I apprenticed for—they all had opinions about how I should live my life. Those opinions were an education in how to make decisions. And in how not to.

In addition to other people's opinions, there were also lessons about making decisions that I internalized from what I was reading, even if the problems posed would not be mine for years. I remember, for example, coming across a reproach attributed to Sophia Tolstoy, who asked her husband, Leo Tolstoy, "How many lives must be burned to keep the fire of genius alive?" Even though I didn't have a wife or children then, her question challenged my dreams anyway. Is there an empathetic person who has pursued a passion with intensity and not been haunted by the question of whether it's worth it, not just for themselves, but for those around them?

Life has resolved many of my early struggles with uncertainty, opinions, and outside influences. I continue to try to make good decisions, but these days I tend to think—echoing T. S. Eliot in *The Four Quartets*—that it is the trying that matters. The rest is not our business, or not a business that should consume us. Most of the time, we only come to understand what was meaningful or necessary through the use we make of our choices and the awareness those choices help bring about. Agonizing over decisions, trying to predict which path will lead to the best outcome, often misses the deeper task: to be as honest and present as we can in the choosing, and then to take responsibility for shaping a meaningful life out of whatever path we've chosen.

Still, even with all this in mind, I'll try to say something about how decisions are made, since that is the question before us.

There is the powerful role of intuition, something we all recognize but struggle to describe. There are also the subtle contextual signals and the information we gather both from our surroundings and from within ourselves. And then there is experience. We make decisions differently when we have encountered a situation before, when we recognize familiar patterns, or when the consequences remind us of what we have been through. Decisions often also draw from tradition, where the wisdom and actions of those before us reveal possibilities for ourselves, but this inheritance is too layered and interconnected to fully explain in a few paragraphs. For example, it is nearly impossible to make a decision as an artist that does not, in some way, engage with tradition, even when we are rejecting that tradition.

I find it helpful to approach systematically and rationally what can be approached that way, which, as time goes on, seems to be less and less. Once I have thought carefully about what a decision is asking of me, inspected the possible consequences, entertained doubts, and made a proper effort to understand the situation contextually, I usually arrive at a sense of what I might need to do. If the decision is familiar or unlikely to alter my life in a significant way (though what truly changes a life is often unpredictable), there is a good chance I will make the right choice by following that sense.

But when a decision is critical, which is more often than we assume, that sense is rarely enough. Once the rational arguments have been laid out, emotions weighed, and doubts considered, a gap remains. To close it, I turn to a part of myself that seems to know what must be done.

Where does this other knowledge come from?

It does not arise from reason, though it does not defy reason. Nor does it come from feeling, though it is not without feeling. Is it shaped by the accumulation of our experiences, the echoes of intuition, or something more elusive and innate, like heart or soul? Whatever its source, this knowledge is not invented but uncovered, like a path concealed until the moment we are ready to walk it. To trust it requires humility, not as an act of virtue but as a necessity. Martin Heidegger might call it openness to Being. Søren Kierkegaard, faith.

This deeper knowledge reveals itself through attention. The quality of attention we bring to a situation shapes what we perceive and, ultimately, what we know. When attention is narrow and driven by the desire for control or certainty, it reduces the complexity of the moment, stripping it of nuance and possibility. In contrast, an open, receptive attention creates space for subtle truths to emerge, truths that resist being forced into view. This kind of attention is alive and active, a way of engaging with the world that accepts and respects its fullness. It asks us to set aside the impulse to control and instead listen to what the moment itself offers.

Some decisions are so significant and complex that our capacity to respond is tested to the point where we feel incapable of resolving them. When faced with overwhelming decisions, I used to make pros and cons lists, read about the issues involved, envision living with one choice versus the other, and, at the end of that process, make a decision that felt educated and rational. Rarely did I allow whimsy or emotion to play a significant role in my considerations.

Now, I trust calculation less than I used to. I still go through that rational process, but I rely on it less. For one thing, it's not as rational as I once believed. I often catch myself looking for evidence that confirms what I already want to do. Then, after that pseudo-rational analysis has run its course, I try to live in the space the decision has opened and let that deeper knowing I mentioned earlier reveal something.

I say "something" because, at times, what is revealed is not the decision itself, but what the decision suggests about that moment in my life. This period of living in the space opened by a decision and influenced by deeper knowing may be brief, but it can be transformative—sometimes in dramatic ways, when desperation and urgency, rather than caution or strategy, dictate the way forward.

As I reread the last few paragraphs, I realize again that what I've tried to describe about how I make decisions isn't especially clear, and perhaps can't be. Much of it unfolds outside the reach of language, shaped by intuition, receptivity, accident, and other ways of knowing that resist explanation. Yet, even in its obscurity, the process feels real and steady enough to trust. The forces and circumstances may change, but the process itself—one involving doubt, acceptance, reasoning, and deep insight, often accompanied by a leap of faith—remains constant across my roles as artist, father, husband, friend, son, citizen, and in the parts of life that elude labels. Every decision is a step forward, accompanied by the effort to remain aware: of oneself, of the act of choosing, and of the movement toward an unknown future that each decision sets in motion.

3

What remains in both your professional and personal life tasks? Obstacles therein?

Just so it's clear—
No whining on the journey.
If you whine, you'll get stuck
Somewhere with people
Like yourself.

Stephen Dunn

EMC: I am in Miami sitting at a table at my brother's house looking at a painting I did in my early twenties. It's of a couple leaning against each other. The man is dressed in a black suit and is wearing an African mask. His hand on the woman's shoulder is possessive, claw-like. She is dressed in red. Some cleavage shows under what might be a pearl necklace. Behind their heads there are vibrating shapes as if energy was emanating from the figures.

There's something derivative about the painting, but it has a presence I wouldn't have expected from an early work, probably because my expectations overlook an obvious fact about my work: the vein I would mine for the next forty years was already there at the beginning. This constancy of sensitivity seems true of most artists, and I think it applies to many inner lives as well. Though it may take different forms over time, a core concern or spirit remains, shaping how we see and what we seek. Mining its richness and following where it leads has taken time, but that vein ultimately defines the heart of my practice. In it, I can best recognize not just what I am, but who I am, and maybe, why I am.

If this enduring thread of concern is real, if a single, evolving current runs through much of what I've done, then what is progress? What does it mean to have accomplished something? And what, really, are obstacles?

We are taught to equate progress with production: with output, acceleration, and measurable success. This mindset pervades nearly every domain, and the art world is no exception. For many artists, gallerists, curators, and collectors, progress has become synonymous with visibility, with success measured in recognition and market value rather than in depth or resonance. The demands of the art world—the pressure to produce, to remain relevant—often distance them from what first made art meaningful. The result is a cycle of self-exploitation: relentless striving that leads not to fulfillment but to detachment, numbness, and cynicism. The pursuit of success, shaped more by external expectations than personal insight, has left many disillusioned.

The Korean-German philosopher Byung-Chul Han has written about this pervasive culture of self-exploitation. He describes how the shift from external disciplinary forces to internalized pressure has led to widespread burnout, anxiety, and depression. Where power structures were once clearly defined—master and slave, ruler and ruled—modern individuals have absorbed both roles, driving themselves to exhaustion in the name of productivity and self-optimization. This internalized struggle turns ambition into oppression, making people complicit in their own subjugation.

Therefore, since so much emphasis is placed on markers of success, the question of what remains—in both our professional and personal life tasks, and the obstacles therein—often leads to reflections shaped by judgment and comparison, guided by external standards. But I prefer to turn the question inward, toward the unfolding of art and life: how far and deep this unfolding has gone, what holds me back, and what it reveals about our place in a greater totality. If borrowed notions of achievement disconnect us from what truly matters, then part of the work is to resist these forces, not by rejecting ambition or effort, but by rooting them in something more fundamental, less transient. To measure progress not by accumulation or validation, but by clarity, depth, and the presence of something alive in the work and in myself. And to see obstacles not as hindrances to be conquered, but as part of the unfolding itself, demanding attention, shaping the path, and revealing why we are on the path in the first place.

This orientation toward presence and a sense of something larger than myself has come slowly, shaped less by conclusions than by the ongoing experience of inquiry, and by the authenticity the process requires, from which humility has gradually emerged. So when it comes to addressing the question posed—*What remains in both your professional and personal life tasks? Obstacles therein?*—I have to start with where I am. And the simplest way to put it, the point from which any answer to what remains, and the obstacles involved, must unfold, is this: I know more than I once did about art and life. Still, I move through both as a novice.

That might sound like a strange claim, given what I've been doing for the past four decades. When I started painting, paint, brushes, and charcoal were tools, something I used, separate from my hand. Now, they use me as much as I use them. I know them as part of me. In the same way, many aspects of the day-to-day life of being an artist have become more familiar, more instinctive. My understanding of how artists have worked in the past has also deepened. Where I once saw only a beautiful passage by the late Titian, I now see the fantastic and mysterious battles between aging and facility, fatigue and urgency, divinity and incompleteness. And alongside the work in the studio, I've spent years reading, writing, and trying to live life as best I could, learning from my mistakes, and, not uncommonly, the same one more than once.

Yet all that has only served to make what once seemed accessible feel more out of reach. That, in part, is where the sense of being a novice comes from, but instead of frustration, I feel gratitude for this remoteness and mystery. It inspires me.

It is imperative for an artist to confront immensity, to feel lost, and then to recognize ourselves as part of something beyond our bodies. As I continue to unfold my work, I find myself drawn to expanding the connection between my life, my practice, and the rhythms of the studio. I already work toward this integration, but in the coming years, I hope to discover more, allowing the boundaries between these spheres to dissolve further.

Writing has long been a deep and necessary part of my process, not just as a form of reflection, but as a parallel practice that informs and expands my work. In my younger days, it was writers, especially Latin American poets and novelists, who offered me an emotional and artistic education I couldn't find elsewhere. They revealed that there was no need to choose between the individual and the world, between human emotion and artistic rigor, between the interior life and social responsibility. Their work allowed for a complexity that embraced beauty, justice, and tenderness without sentimentality. That understanding shaped not only how I came to art but what I expected of it. That early influence stayed with me, shaping the questions I returned to and the way I approached my own work. Over the years, in addition to the writing that emerges within the studio process, I've published several books of poetry, essays, and reflections. And now, with an upcoming novel, I see literature as another space of inquiry and expansion.

Beyond my own practice, I often think about the ways art circulates: how it is experienced, how it is acquired, and how it is still too often confined to an elite. Teaching has been one way to counter this limitation, but I continue to seek opportunities to bring the values and sensitivities of my work into everyday life. I have designed houses, gardens, institutional spaces, and furniture as environments that shape how we live. In the same spirit, I'm interested in collaborating with designers to extend my practice into what people wear, bringing the concerns of my work into the textures and forms that move through the world. These are ways of carrying my work beyond the gallery or the collector's home, creating experiences that invite presence, care, and a more attentive way of living.

I struggle with the dissonance between spending months striving for something authentic and transformative, only to have that work enter the machinery of commerce, where it's judged by trends, collector preferences, and speculative value. But I'm grateful that I can earn a living from my work, which few artists can do. Most rely on other jobs—teaching, working in restaurants or offices, doing construction, even forging antiquities. Historically, some of the best-known artists also had outside sources of income: Van Gogh relied on his brother; Ai Weiwei was a blackjack dealer; Rothko, Guston, and others taught; Jackson Pollock sold baby carriages. The idea that creative work should exist independent of other means of support is a fantasy for most, sustained by an art market that privileges a few and obscures the realities of the rest.

For those of us who do make a living as artists, the pressures are different but no less compromising. The work must sell, the galleries must show it, collectors must buy it, curators must include it, critics must write about it, and auction prices must hold. The market, for all its flaws, allows us to keep working by providing materials, resources, and time in the studio, yet it also distorts. It rewards certain kinds of work, creates hierarchies of visibility, and applies an economic logic to something that, at its best, resists commodification. Trends emerge and disappear, collectors speculate, institutions reinforce existing structures, and all the while, the artist is left to wonder whether the work remains true or has begun to bend—maybe imperceptibly—toward what is expected, what is rewarded. Some accept this reality, treating the system as part of their practice. Others resist, seeking ways to step outside it. But where is the line between integrity and compromise, and is it fixed or shifting? At what point does survival become complicity, or simply the cost of staying in the world?

Another obstacle in an art practice is the image we construct of ourselves, which often becomes a constraint on reinvention and transition. This self-imposed structure shapes the choices we make, our sense of identity as artists, and the circles we engage with. It also manifests in what we call our style or voice. Because this version of ourselves took years and effort to build, it's natural to want to preserve it. Yet growth sometimes depends on letting go of this construction. The persona we create is not just a public mask, but a framework that governs how we see ourselves, move through the world, and define what is possible. Formed over time through habit, reinforcement, and necessity, it determines the roles we assume, the risks we take, and the limits we accept. Eventually, it ceases to feel like a construct and becomes a shell we mistake for who we are, one we rarely question even as it shapes not only how we live but also what we allow ourselves to dream.

Perhaps no story captures this more clearly than that of Narcissus. He dies at the water's edge, but the real death comes long before. He has no need for others, no room for love or change. He stares into the pool, trapped by his own image, unable to turn away, unable to step beyond what he knows. It isn't vanity that ruins him, but the refusal to let go of who he believes himself to be. He wastes away not from hunger or thirst, but from the failure to move, to shift, to make space for something beyond the reflection. This is the danger: to hold too tightly to the person we have constructed, to mistake it for something final. To do so is to stop growing, and what no longer grows begins, in some way, to die.

It's disconcertingly easy to keep adding layers to that shell until we become a hardened, garden-statue version of ourselves. The tendency to become fixed in our ways, to mistake our achievements and habits for who we are, becomes a practical concern as life accumulates. We all carry the weight of these identities, shaped by work, recognition, failure, and expectation, gradually solidifying in ways we don't always notice. There are moments when the shell cracks—through loss, dissatisfaction, or a shift in circumstance. Sometimes it's a passing comment or a moment of discomfort; other times, a catastrophe. These moments are unsettling because they strip away certainty, but they also open the possibility for change.

If we can recognize our persona as something we created rather than something we are, we might loosen its grip, allowing for reinvention not as a forced act but as a necessary evolution. To hold too tightly to a fixed identity is to risk stagnation, to become a curator of a past self rather than someone actively shaping a life. The challenge is not to abandon what we have built, but to discern what is fundamental from what is merely familiar, what remains essential and what has simply become habit. The structures we build, and the version of ourselves shaped through them, offer stability and rewards but also impose limits. Loosening them, even slightly, requires trust in the possibility that there is still room to become. This evolution is not easy. There's a natural fear of losing our identity, and we all deceive ourselves at times about who we are and what we need. Sometimes we're simply doing our best to hold life together. Many have built their persona as protection from pain, loss, or abuse, and questioning it can understandably feel frightening. Often, we need help or guidance to face the image we've constructed, especially when it no longer serves us.

I don't have a formula for confronting the shell, the edifice, the garden statue I've built, but I know that effort and attention matter, and that relying on those closest to me, on reality observed as deeply as I can manage, on art, and on a voice within makes a difference. My family and friends, whether through their insight or their frustrations, and the reflections that loss brings remind me of what remains unseen in myself. Communion with nature offers another measure, stripping away pretense, dissolving boundaries, restoring proportion, and offering inspiration. And then there is the leap that art sometimes makes possible—the moment when something emerges that bypasses the known self and opens a door I didn't realize was there.

JH: The famous story of the Damoclean sword reminds us that the path ahead of us is never to be presumed, never certain at all. A tire rolled off a truck on the other side of a median, bounced across into the lane ahead, and through the window of a colleague of mine. In an instant he became a paraplegic, losing mobility, losing his spouse, and losing all the plans they had for a life together. Further, our capacity to plan ahead is also frequently a matter of the context of the hour. For my good friend Enrique we trust there are many miles to go before he sleeps, *Deo volente*, and he is probably just entering the peak of his professional, and possibly, personal life. At eighty-five, medically compromised, and living in a retirement facility, the vista appears rather more constrained in this wheelhouse. Yet, my mind still works, my imagination still riots, and there is a quickened spirit ready for the next stage of this journey. I have always been moved by those lines from Tennyson's *Ulysses*:

> How dull it is to pause, to make an end,
> To rust unburnished, not to shine in use!
> As though to breathe were life! Life piled on
> life

Were all too little, and of one to me
Little remains; but every hour is saved
From that eternal silence…
Old age hath yet his honor and his toil.
Death closes all; but something ere the end,
Some work of noble note, may yet be done,
Not unbecoming men that strove with gods.

While a part of me wanted to put my feet up on the couch and watch the ballgame or read a spy novel, a much larger part quickened when Enrique proposed this book. Even though the tempter Indolence resisted, followed by that seductress Distraction, they were quickly over-ruled by, yes, the little people within. (Jung once said that without the quickening of the spirit, humankind would indulge in its greatest vice: Indolence. And we all live in a noisy culture whose chief promise to us is daily diversion.) I probably tergiversated only a day or so before agreeing to the project. Not only did I look forward to deepening our relationship, I was curious to see what might come out of such a dialogue in the face of the questions we pose ourselves herein. And frankly, I would not look forward to the nagging and sullen attitudes I would have to face if I overruled the little people within. I have experienced that enough times and do not wish to contend with them again.

Professionally, I do not feel I have anything I need to prove, nor any mountain to climb. Yet, my work through the years reminds me that there is always another layer beneath the layer just uncovered. There is always something to enlarge this inner journey, even as the experience of aging diminishes the outer journey. I do not miss airports or waiting for the pickup at a hotel any more though I do miss seeing friends acquired along the way. Thank goodness for Zoom which has allowed mobility in the presence of disability. As annoying as computers can be, I love internet search engines that take us to places we could not visit in any case, access information we would never be able to find in the local library, and converse with people in distant places about diverse matters.

The real challenges remaining for me are found on the personal front. While I have as strong a desire to keep living as the next person, I have for some time considered these last couple of years, post-surgeries, post-cancers, as a bonus, an appendix, or a coda not granted my son, or my brother, or to numerous friends who have passed. Moreover, apart from wafting on the winds of the inherent life force, I think my chief personal raison d'être is to be here for my wife. At our last anniversary, she gave me a card that had one sentence on it: *"Someday you'll find this card in a drawer and we will still be in love."* So, you get the idea. I am continuing to look forward to our unfolding journey together, however long it lasts, but, further, she needs me to help her in the face of her own medical and mobility challenges. Plus, I am still curious, and curiosity drives my internal engine.

We need to remember that we, statistically, live much longer than our predecessors. My father lost his mother and two little brothers in 1932 from diphtheria. The average age of mortality in North America in 1900 was forty-seven, and longevity in the United States in 1935 when Social Security was created was sixty-seven, hence the program was only supposed to last two years, which helps account for why the program is in chronic fiscal trouble. As a moment in history, we all profit from cleaner water supply (considered by some experts the single biggest improvement in longevity in human history), the invention of miracle drugs and much more sophisticated forms of surgery and pain palliation. So, what have we to complain about? As a recent beneficiary of radiation, chemotherapy, and surgery, I am grateful for modern medicine and grieve what my ancestors had to face. When I rise in the morning, I do not know whether the wires linking my spine to my pelvis will hold one more day or not, but the outcome of that issue is above my pay grade. My job is to get up, shut up, and suit up, as best I can. My job includes living with chronic pain without complaining, and with every outer diminishment to continue to grow within. As W. B. Yeats wrote in "Sailing to Byzantium,"

> An aged man is but a paltry thing,
> A tattered coat upon a stick, unless
> Soul clap its hands and sing, and louder sing
> For every tatter in its mortal dress.

Plato believed that the considered life included the daily contemplation of mortality, not as a morbid preoccupation, but rather as a reminder that one's choices matter, that one is not here for long, and as an encouragement to live for something more than fear or self-absorption. There are many ways of dying and death is only one of them. We die when fear dominates our choices; we die when we choose security over growth; we die when we forget that we are accountable for how we live our lives.

Since so many of us are living so much longer, may we enquire if longevity itself is the goal, or is it something else? Are our lives four times richer, more meaningful, than those who lived in ancient Greece, or twice richer, more meaningful, than those who lived just a century ago? Will those who live longer into this present century live better lives, and how would we know that? How do we define "better," by "longevity"? Finally… Finally, why *should* we live longer—just because our neuroses say so? Or our ego whines, "because I want to?" And does the universe agree with our conclusions? Freud was heroic around this. While in the terminal phase of his cancer of the jaw, having no belief in an afterlife, he observed that his removal from life would have minimal consequence because he had contributed the piece of the puzzle of which he was capable, and had nothing further to say. He was, it would seem, able to accept his end with equanimity, courage, and finality. I hope to emulate him in this shared journey into the unknown.

While the question of an afterlife much preoccupied me in the first half of life, I find the question not very pressing these days. I once was, as young people are, identified with our conscious ego world. Today, much less so. I do not know if there is an afterlife, nor do I find myself caring very much either way. If there is another life, then it is *another* life, and not this one. If so, it is far more mysterious than this poor mind can imagine. And if it is only effacement, annihilation, then any present contentions are rendered moot, irrelevant. I am today comfortable in saying I do not know, and I don't care very much. In either case, I no longer think *I* need to be perpetuated.

Meanwhile, I intend no disrespect whatsoever to the affirmations of faith in an afterlife, but I do ask that we simply not consider it a closed question, and therefore avoid the great depth and complexity to which our life always summons us. On the one hand we have a long cultural history of belief in an afterlife, and on the other hand we have the equally fervent denial of its existence by many others. If you ask my opinion, it is only an opinion, and matters very little. Rationally, I suspect we are scattered to the winds of the cosmos; intuitively, I imagine some form of spiritual continuation. Which one prevails is subject to the velleities of the moment. But there is a middle ground here, one which respects and tolerates mystery and also honors the symbolic images which emerge autonomously from our psyche. But I do believe that my task now is to continue to observe and respect the images that arise from the depths and to explore the new refractive lenses through which we might see the mystery of it all from a different angle.

The greatest, perduring affront to the sovereign fantasies of the human ego is its perishability—the fact of which is profoundly inscribed in and unfolding through the eschatology of our cells during each moment of this querulous, quarrelsome journey. All rising things fall; all ascendant things return to earth; all bodies in motion submit to the law of entropy. The pragmatic question which confronts us, then, is: *what does this fact make us do*, or *keep us from doing?* And how might we live more *abundantly* in the presence of our mortality? And, finally, does mortality even matter? The core idea in this chapter is that an aroused awareness of mortality is not the same as fear of mortality. Daily, we are summoned to be mindful of mortality in order not to tumble into triviality, or be unconsciously governed by fear of that which is our most natural fact.

In the first half of life, our ego is shaped by discerning what the world wants of us, and either meeting those demands or fleeing them. At this stage of the journey, it is less about what my tiny ego wants in this star-flung universe and much more about continuing to be a vehicle for what wants to enter through me, as a person, as a therapist, as a partner, as a writer. Rather than whine, we might be grateful that that brings us steady employment, at least for now. Thus, this life stage still asks us to serve the life force that has carried us up till now. In this way we honor both the mystery and contribute our small chip to the grand mosaic.

As we return to "Ulysses," we know that for this hour, if not beyond that, the vessel puffs its sail. And while the deep moans around with many voices, the tide is about to turn and we have to catch the current that will take us out there on the high seas.

> Though much is taken, much abides; and though
> We are not now that strength which in old days
> Moved earth and heaven, that which we are, we are.

4

What are the risks, setbacks, shadow issues that rose/rise from your vocation? Mistakes? Defeats?

In the middle, not only in the middle of the way
But all the way, in a dark wood, in a bramble,
On the edge of a grimpen, where is no secure foothold,
And menaced by monsters, fancy lights,
Risking enchantment. Do not let me hear
Of the wisdom of old men, but rather of their folly,
Their fear of fear and frenzy, their fear of possession,
Of belonging to another, or to others, or to God.
The only wisdom we can hope to acquire
Is the wisdom of humility: humility is endless.
T.S. Eliot

JH: First I have to interrogate myself in discerning: what is my *vocation*? Most of us hold many jobs in our lifetime. I specifically recall laboring in a dairy, working on a tractor/grader assembly line, painting dorm rooms through college and graduate school, cleaning houses, teaching, starting professional education all over, therapist, public speaker, administrator, and numerous others. I do not consider any of them a mistake or a setback. Each was necessary at the time, and from each I learned something. But only one has been a central thread: teacher. And that has been my vocation all along.

From my earliest years in public school, I admired my teachers as they opened doors for me, addressed my questions, and affirmed me in my curiosity. They were mostly older ladies, including one local public librarian who early on told me I did not have to stay in the children's section of the library but could roam everywhere. (She knew a reader when she saw one.) What a gift that was. Years later when I wrote a book of my own, I hunted her down to thank her and found that she had moved from the city library to the State of Illinois library. I hope I was able to alert her to my gratitude in opening the door to the journey not only of a larger life but also of the imagination to go beyond. I suspect I was sometimes, okay, perhaps often, annoying to others of my playmates for I felt an obligation, a sacred duty almost, to share what I was learning with them. If I found it so rich and valuable, why would I not want to share that experience with them?

But all along, there was a shadow issue coursing beneath the surface of things, a Great White in search of a leg to pull under. But more about that soon. For all this interest in learning, perhaps teaching, I had only mediocre grades throughout high school and might not have made it to college had I not had high verbals on the exams. When I entered college, I had no idea what I wanted to do, so I considered being a journalist because I knew that they wrote. Writing books seemed unthinkable at that time. For the first two years, my grades followed their desultory path, subordinate to playing football which I loved. (And do to this day, though I have grown so much more ambivalent as we learn the damage these young men do to their bodies.) Once, while moving as a defensive half-back toward tackling the ball-carrier, I was hit from the side and felt my ligament pull and snap. Over that spring break I had surgery to repair that damage. When the surgeon came in after, he told me that he found multiple pieces of bone in there, that I had some sort of genetic bone disorder, and that by the time I was forty I would not likely be walking. In the twelve days in the hospital thereafter I entered the first dark night: what to do with myself. Lying there as the sophomore (etymologically, "wise fool") that I was, it finally occurred to me: "Well… I am in college, so I could become a student." What stunning sagacity! The grades took off after that. And, thanks to my good fortune, and their gracefulness, several faculty rallied around and supported my entering graduate school. And a little before the twenty-seventh birthday, I had finished my doctorate in literature and philosophy. Shortly after that, I had the highest joy of becoming a parent, a role I still cherish.

I loved those early years teaching because teaching was even more a chance to keep learning. As the old saying has it, you don't really know anything till you can teach it to another. All, then, was moving along predictably, wonderfully, as it was supposed to do with a planned life, or so I believed. And in the mid-thirties, that large thing in the depths below came lurching upward and swallowed me in a life-threatening depression. The short version of those troubled years ultimately led me from the life of a quasi-intellectual through the dark night of the soul to my present world as a Jungian psychoanalyst, teacher, and author.

While I have written more about the in-between emotional travail, the subject assigned here is rather to address the risks, setbacks, and shadow issues that stood in the way, and still do. What I could not have known until the autonomy of the psyche pulled me under was that I had built so much of that first half of life structure in reaction to the circumstances of that stage, and however sincere I was, that much of it was an elaborate effort to transcend, deny, assuage the demons within. Having already declared that my life-long vocation was the pursuit and enjoyment of the systole-diastole of learning and teaching, I could not have fathomed how much of the life I had constructed, what D. W. Winnecott called "the false self," was built over a yawning crevasse of fear, shame, a gnawing sense of unworthiness, and intimidation by it all. As a child, I knew that my mother and father had had very difficult lives. My mother was an orphan. Her father, a Swedish immigrant, died in a coal mine collapse and her mother was a seamstress. Throughout school she had dresses made of flower sacks which her mother had sewn for her, and she lived a life of shame and indigence. When economic hard times came, my father was pulled out of grade school at age thirteen and sent to work for the rest of his life. While he never complained, but shouldered his fate stoically, I knew that his soul had been deeply violated. From them I learned caring, yes, but also avoidance, huddling together for mutual protection, shame, lack of permission to desire what life might bring, and a generalized fear of the world "out there." I have nothing but gratitude for their sacrifices, compassion for their sufferings, and love for their presence, but their child dreamed of flying aboard the occasional plane that flew overhead, someday seeing the ocean with its reported waves, and getting some answers to the questions that troubled me.

Quite separately, and owing perhaps to the recondite gods that bring us to this turbulent planet, I was and perhaps remain an overly sensitive child. I think many children are. But, growing up as a child during WWII, overtly safe in America's heartland, and surrounded by people who would have died for me, I internalized the fear, the grief, the suffering of others. Many times I would climb a tree to be alone, or go to a corner of the block, and sing songs on behalf of those others in peril out there. Such songs included "Now is the Hour," "We'll Meet Again," "Bluebirds Over the White Cliffs of Dover," and strangely, "Home on the Range." Popular during WWII, these were songs of solidarity with others whom I had not met but from what I heard, and seen, were suffering.

I mention these two areas of childhood experience, the generalized fear and depression of both my family of origin, and a civilization aflame with maniacal violence, as the twin currents that fed what became a large shadow for me. Jung's concept of the "shadow" includes our capacity for evil to be sure, but it also includes our unlived possibilities. Generically, the shadow is the embodiment of those aspects of ourselves, or our institutional affiliations, that when brought into consciousness, is intimidating to us, threatening us, or contradictory to our professed values. If, as the ancient playwright Terence observed, nothing human is alien to us, then it obliges the fragile and permeable ego to have to deal with, or not deal with, those contents that are so contradictory or challenging to us.

Having reported in the paragraphs above how angst-ridden home life was, and how troubled the world was, I slowly learned to cope by that most primitive of defenses, denial, and by distancing. Additionally, my Jungian typology is that of an introverted intuitive thinker. As an introvert, I internalized nearly everything, except sports, and even there I sometimes I let other players win because I did not want them to feel bad. As an intuitive, the membrane between me and the world was quite permeable. And as a thinker, I could intellectualize what I had witnessed or felt. All of this, allied with my love of learning, led me, despite those early dismal grades when I was bored with matters and reading on the outside, to gain admittance to the proverbial ivory tower. I prided myself on distancing myself from my feelings. It is not that I was lacking them; they were all too present, too threatening. Is it then any wonder that that Great White was circling beneath the surface waiting to grab that boy's errant leg?

When the depression arrived with those neglected riches buried beneath the sea, the result was an overthrow of the false self. I was prone to self-harm out of self-loathing, and during those dark days I know I brought harm to others. My initial hours of therapy in America led me to several years of analysis at the Jung Institute in Zürich. My first dream, the one I took to my first hour there, was a classic. I was a knight on the ramparts of a medieval castle. The air was thick with arrows as the walls of that fortified self was under siege. At the edge of a forest I saw that the assault was directed by a witch figure, an embodiment of the repressed anima energies, a man's feeling, instinctual, relational and spiritual life. What else would one expect from the regions down below, an engraved invitation to another seminar on the life of the mind? Shortly thereafter, I also had an intra-psychic visitation by a huge, bear-like creature informing me that he would help me find "the child" I had left behind so many years ago. Who would make this sort of thing up? They were images rising from the folks within, the compensatory energies seeking healing and greater investment of energy. It was one of my many lessons that taught me that the human psyche, when listened to, and respected, is seeking to heal itself.

While I did not undertake those years in analysis to find a new "job," I did discover that the conversation with the soul could go on in so many deeper and more satisfying forms than I could find in the classroom I have taught at the college or graduate level for sixty years now, since I was twenty-five, and valued all of it, but the most satisfying teaching has come after employing the frame of analytic psychology that asks what normally is not present in academic inquiry, an interrogation that involves the unconscious: from whence has this come, really, and what is its purpose, really? (I have to add that word *really* because complexes have such wily ways of distracting the fragile ego from whatever might overthrow its management systems.)

During my psychiatric internship, I shuttled some days between the conversations transpiring on the academic campus with those occurring in a locked ward of a state psychiatric hospital. At night, I often wrote "poems" to help me process the magnitude of suffering I encountered during the day. While long lost through multiple geographic moves, those poems were a form for release, for insight, and for psychic enlargement. I called the collection *Narrenshiff,* or *Ship of Fools,* referencing the boats or towers in which the "mad" had once been interred. (And we staff were aboard this same rocking vessel as well. This shuttling between campuses caused me to question where madness, self-deception, and radical honesty might best be found.) I found the hospital more disturbing, but more richly authentic than those engagements elsewhere, and slowly this gravitational pull caused me to leave behind a treasured tenured position for the uncertainties of private practice. I have never looked back. The teaching, and the learning, had simply shifted from one audience to another.

Still another shadow issue that affects not only my work but a great many in the "helping professions," whether medicine, social work, clergy, nursing, or another, fall under the rubric of "the wounded healer." Studies have indicated that children growing up in stressed or dysfunctional families frequently conclude that their well-being lies in sacrificing many of their own needs on behalf of "fixing" the family system. Freud noted that the family system is usually dominated by its most damaged member, and seldom is that the child. Such individuals believe, if only partly consciously, that if they can fix the system, then it might finally be there for themselves. As we know, a child cannot heal an adult but attending the family systems can still warp its own developmental agenda. Thus, such adults carry a deep, archaic programming that obliges them to carry on that "calling" in later phases of life. Some of them turn out to be gifted healers, if they have integrated what they need to learn for themselves, but many professional "helpers" suffer burn out, fatigue, depression, and self-medication as their work binds them to that traumatic and disabling past. Through the years I have spoken over 100 times to professional groups describing the etiology, the typical profile of the wounded healer, and the need for a more effective self-care system, up to and including finding another "calling."

The etiology of the wounded healer lurks within me, and allied with that hyper-sensitivity I described above, puts me as much at risk as any. Teaching and writing about it helps. Further, well over half of my practice over the last five decades has been composed of people in the helping professions. So, I get daily reminders of the risk/reward ratio of staying open to the wounds of others without being further pathologized by those intimate encounters. Nonetheless, one of the risk pathologies of the wounded healer is that one never feels off-duty. Since one never leaves one's history behind, that material is continuously evoked. And it is my job to process it, not avoid it or be defined by it.

When I ask myself if I would better off back in academia, the answer is still "no" because I have come to treasure the depth at which analysis moves. More of me is engaged there, and despite the stresses, the richness of that shared experience seems to me full of heart, full of spirit, and full of soul.

EMC: When I think of my vocation, I see myself as an artist. In my understanding of what that means, I include the curiosity about the world and the pursuit of truth that drew me to physics and philosophy, as well as my admiration for literature's ability to illuminate the complexity of the human condition. But to say that my vocation is to be an artist means something less definite than when I used to say I was a scientist. Unlike physics, art is a term so broadly and inconsistently applied to actions and objects whose quality, attitude, and allegiances vary so greatly as to be vague at best. So before turning to the risks, setbacks, and shadow issues that arise from my vocation, I feel it is necessary to explain what I mean by art and, in turn, what I mean by being an artist.

There are things and activities that, while expressive, touching, interesting, innovative, or meaningful to the person who made them and to others, are not experiences I would describe as art—at least not if I am also to use the term for the experience brought forth by a work of Diego Velázquez, for instance. As I see it, an experience is art when it opens a space where truth can unfold, however fragmentary or elusive that truth may be. Not just any truth, but one that moves us emotionally and intellectually, and does so sufficiently enough to bring about a transcendent experience that dissolves the separation between us and the world, even if only briefly. This is not what many people expect from art. It is more common to seek transformative experiences in religion or nature, turning to art instead as an opportunity to be edified or entertained. These varying expectations, together with art's resistance to definition, create confusion about what we call art and how we judge its value.

The experience of art, like all transcendent experiences, eludes explanation, frustrating our impulse to establish rules for what art is. To respond to this, a different kind of assessment is necessary—one that recognizes the ineffable nature and non-discursive quality of artistic experience without allowing that recognition to discourage our expectation of clarity and transcendence. Confusion, rather than clarity, is often the result of the tension between the resistance of art to formulas and our desire to have a clear path to follow. In a vocation where approval, degrees, good intentions, plans, previous experience, and social virtue offer no assurance that our work will open that space where truth and transcendence can unfold, it is easy to get lost. And yet, that uncertainty—the absence of guarantees—is inseparable from what it means to live one's vocation as an artist.

There is no inherent shame in being lost. To be lost while remaining attentive and open may be the only way to reach a place we have not yet been. The reminder, sometimes attributed to Jung, that "if the path before you is clear, you are probably on someone else's," underscores the connection between authenticity and uncertainty, and being an artist means accepting that condition without grasping for familiar tropes or known paths. Even so, artists, feeling disoriented, often trade their confusion for denial or hubris, or lapse into disenchantment and self-doubt, fearing that their lack of certainty makes them impostors. The discomfort of laboring without certainty drives others to seek the reassurance of external validation and the illusion that cleverness, novelty, or intellectual agility can stand in for what truly matters. And yet it is precisely uncertainty, and the confusion that arises when standards and explanations fail, that sustains the artistic process rather than interrupts it. If accepted rather than resisted, feeling lost can strip away assumptions, dismantle illusions, and force us to question what we thought we knew.

This is why the vocation of an artist requires faith, not in a doctrine but in the process itself, in the belief that meaning is not imposed but discovered, and that the experience we seek must be allowed to emerge rather than be forced into being. To live this vocation meaningfully is to recognize that confusion and failure are not obstacles to be avoided but essential conditions of the work. Like most risks, setbacks, and defeats, they are not incidental to the life of an artist but central to it. They arise not only from external circumstances such as lack of recognition, financial instability, and the unpredictability of success, but also from the internal demands of the work and the transformations they bring in us.

Another risk of the vocation is self-deception, the possibility of mistaking effort for meaning, cleverness for depth, or external validation for confirmation of value. All of us lie to ourselves, and artists are especially prone to believe that hard work guarantees significance, that novelty ensures importance, or that recognition proves worth. But none of these are necessarily true. The most disciplined practice can still lead to empty work, and the most widely praised efforts can still fail to create depth and resonance. Artists can—often without realizing it—begin shaping their work to fit the expectations of others, whether those of the market or of their own idea of relevance.

There is also the danger of stagnation, of settling into habits and producing work that is lifeless, repeating past successes without bringing forth anything new. Many careers attest to this. The discipline required to sustain an artistic practice over time can, if one is not vigilant, harden into repetition, generating pastiches of what once were ambitious works. I often think of Giorgio de Chirico in this regard. Early in his career, de Chirico produced haunting, dreamlike cityscapes filled with eerie light, suggestions of lonesome winds, empty streets, and enigmatic figures. His work influenced the Surrealists, and his early paintings remain among the masterpieces of modern art. When I was younger, he was one of my favorites, and some of his paintings remain vivid in my mind. Yet after his early success, de Chirico grew disillusioned with modernism and began to reject his own artistic innovations. He turned toward a more classical, academic style, producing works that lacked the mystery and depth of his earlier paintings. In his later career, he often repeated those early metaphysical works, occasionally backdating them to pass as originals from that period. Although there are interesting aspects to his later work, it lacks the power of his early paintings, and his hostility toward the modern art world (which was not without merit) left him somewhat isolated.

No artist should expect a career without setbacks and periods of uninspired work. Some ideas take years to unfold, requiring patience and persistence without any assurance that they will succeed. Some works fail, whether because they were not strong enough to begin with or because something significant was lost along the way. And there are many times when strong work is met with indifference or misunderstanding, when the gap between what we perceive the work to be and how it is received feels insurmountable. In an art world that relies on markets, tastemakers, and fashions, not everything that should be seen will be seen, and not everything that is powerful will be recognized as such. To continue working under these conditions requires cockroach-like resilience, so it's not surprising that many artists quit after a few years.

Beyond the practical challenges, there are deeper shadow issues that emerge from the vocation itself.

The ego is always present—the temptation to believe in one's own importance, to seek affirmation, or to posture intellectually in ways that mask insecurity. There is also the danger of disillusionment, of becoming cynical in response to the workings of the art world, or of allowing exhaustion and frustration to drain the urgency from one's practice. And then there is the fear that none of it matters, that the pursuit itself is built on illusion, that one has mistaken personal obsession for necessity.

In my own career, I have faced many of these risks and shadow issues. As an artist, past successes, knowledge, and discipline offer little assurance that the work taking shape in the studio will amount to anything meaningful. A work of art that hopes to bring about a transformative experience must necessarily operate in a territory where assurances have long vanished, so we persevere with intuition, awareness, attention, and presence—each subtle and vulnerable to misunderstanding and confusion, making it easy to drift far off course. Sometimes I have found myself lost in superficial pursuits or uplifted into delusions by successful exhibitions. At other moments, when a project fails to receive much attention or when sales thin out, making it harder to sustain my studio and support my family, I have been tempted to withdraw, not from art, but from its public dimension. None of these struggles have held me for long, but tomorrow may be the day I get stuck.

Defeats are a part of the vocation, not separate from it. Some works never get where I hope to take them. Certain ideas, after months or years of effort, lead nowhere, and some aspirations will always remain out of reach. Yet the greatest defeat most artists fear is not the failure of a particular work, but the loss of conviction—the dulling of the inner urgency that compels us to continue. Art is a vocation where progress is often unclear and certainty rare, yet it demands the ability to work within this uncertainty, often without knowing whether what has been done is enough. To accept risks, setbacks, and defeats is a necessary part of an art practice. In fact, this acceptance is largely what it means to be an artist. The greatest challenge is not to avoid these difficulties, but to navigate them without losing one's spirit. There is no way to secure oneself against doubt or eliminate failure, and no guarantee that even the best efforts will be recognized or understood. The calling of the artist is to move forward honestly and with devotion, accepting uncertainty and all the beautiful hostilities that arise from the effort, in order to bring forth an artistic experience that moves us emotionally while offering clarity and connection.

5

What does resilience mean to you, and in what ways has it shaped your journey in life and work? Are there moments that defined or challenged your resilience?

In the midst of winter, I found there was, within me, an invincible summer. And that makes me happy. For it says that no matter how hard the world pushes against me, within me, there's something stronger—something better, pushing right back.

Albert Camus

EMC: My mother and father were born and raised in a small rural town on Cuba's Caribbean shore. My father lost his father as a child and began working in his teens to support his mother and sisters, first cutting sugar cane and later repairing equipment at the sugar mill, despite having no formal engineering education. My mother came from a wealthy family and, unlike her siblings who all went into medicine, became a teacher because it was my grandfather's dream. Both lived through the Cuban Revolution, which upended the life they had known and brought despair to both families while they were still teenagers. Then, in their early twenties, just after completing the house my father had built through the hardships and shortages imposed by the new government and the American embargo, they had two children while still, in many ways, barely more than children themselves. They came from a society that demanded an early adoption of an adult persona while ignoring or resisting the internal growth needed to make it authentic and sustaining.

Opposed to communism and facing the harsh realities of rural Cuba, they applied to leave the country, entering a protracted and painful purgatory that lasted several years before eventually migrating to Franco's Spain—my father first, then, two years later, my mother, my brother, and me. In Madrid, my family, now with three children, faced the financial and social struggles common to many immigrants, intensified by the conditions of a totalitarian and economically depressed country. While my mother was still in her late twenties and my father in his early thirties, we emigrated to Puerto Rico. Rather than the good life they had hoped for, in the new island we faced economic and social setbacks so frequent and severe that, if I were to tell the full story, it would seem unbelievable. I can't recall all the jobs and fledgling businesses they had, but I would guess there were more than thirty, most of them my father's, ranging from construction, to selling used motors, to delivering bread. My mother had only seven: putting caps on milk bottles, assembling custom jewelry, teaching elementary school, selling jewelry door-to-door, making food to sell, working at several of my father's businesses, and starting a small preschool.

It is hard to imagine having seven businesses, and even harder to imagine dozens, patenting four inventions, and seeing them all fail, as happened to my father. And it is inconceivable to think this happened while raising three boys in two foreign countries, without any safety nets. Yet, it is not unusual for immigrants to scramble into a double-digit number of jobs or hustle-driven ventures. Without money, networks, education, or a clear understanding of the realities of a new country, but facing closed doors and the need to survive, they become resourceful in finding ways to make a living.

Having experienced that history, I took it as a matter of course that people would get up again after being crushed by failure, bankruptcy, robbery, bullying, and betrayal, because that was what I saw my parents do again and again. Then, at some point in my twenties, I realized how remarkable it was that they kept starting over each time a promising effort fell apart. All these efforts followed a similar arc: first came the idea, then the excitement and visions of its potential, followed by the name—often pieced together from fragments of Catholic virgins' names. When a place was needed, our meager savings were spent or money was borrowed, and whatever construction was required, we did ourselves. This enthusiastic period was wonderful but short, and the gradual demise, painful and protracted. We learned something from each disaster, and my mother, eventually striking out on her own, started a preschool that has endured for about forty years.

For me, that history reflects colossal endurance and a heroic capacity to keep going, and I admire my parents for never giving up. I also feel deep compassion and gratitude for the price they paid for their daring journey. Without a doubt, the story of my family, and especially my parents, is one of the strength of the human spirit, the drive to survive, and the sacrifices we make for those we love. It is a story of loyalty, strength, desperation, endurance, and stubbornness.

But it is not a story of resilience.

Resilience is often mistaken for sheer endurance: the ability to withstand difficulty without breaking. But to me, it has more to do with how one continues—what is carried forward, what is left behind, and the clarity that emerges in the process. It is not just persistence but the ongoing negotiation between holding on and letting go.

In Ernest Hemingway's *A Farewell to Arms*, after witnessing loss, betrayal, and the destruction of war, Lieutenant Frederic Henry reflects on the indiscriminate nature of suffering, reinforcing Hemingway's themes of disillusionment and life's indifference:

> The world breaks everyone and afterward many are strong at the broken places. But those that will not break it kills. It kills the very good and the very gentle and the very brave impartially. If you are none of these you can be sure it will kill you too but there will be no special hurry.

That strength in the broken places, which echoes Nietzsche's maxim, "Out of life's school of war: what doesn't kill you makes you stronger," is often not the strength that enriches the spirit and provides visions of a wider life's landscape. Instead, it is the strength of knowing one can survive, which while powerful and sometimes a source of confidence, is all too often accompanied by darkness, suspicion, disenchantment, and tiredness. What my parents went through broke them in critical ways that maimed their spirit, and we, their children, have had to work hard—and are still working—not to be broken by that history as well. I don't know if I could have handled it any better, and it is likely I would have come through that history worse, more wounded, less intact than they did. Despite their strength, patience, and in no small way, heroism, the weight of their struggles took something significant from them. They endured, but endurance alone is not the same as resilience. Their hardships rarely led to healing and, in the end, left them carrying the burdens of bitterness and resentment, seeing more of the failures and mistakes than their remarkable accomplishments.

Resilience requires recalibration, the ability to integrate failure, disillusionment, and pain in a way that fosters a different, perhaps clearer, engagement with the world. It implies an internal shift, however small, not just enduring hardship but being shaped by it, deepening understanding, sharpening perception, or reinforcing a sense of meaning. Hardship is not an enemy. Suffering is not something to be conquered but something to be borne. Resilience is not about pushing away what comes but about meeting it as it is, without grasping or retreating.

More than mere persistence, resilience is the capacity to withstand and adapt to challenges, setbacks, and uncertainty without losing integrity and without destroying one's spirit. It is not rigidity but flexibility, the willingness to reassess, to release what no longer serves, and to move forward with clarity rather than blind determination.

There have been times when resilience felt like defiance—choosing to continue despite failure, sadness, and uncertainty. Other times, it felt like surrender, like recognizing when to let go of what had lost meaning. The balance between holding on and letting go is never fixed or final, and often, it is only in retrospect that I understand which was needed. Resilience is an aim, not a fixed state, and often it is imperfect, clumsy. Fear overtakes clarity, exhaustion sets in, and I falter. That, too, is part of it. To persist does not mean being unshaken but continuing while shaken, uncertain, or when the effort feels insufficient. What matters is not flawless endurance but the willingness to begin again, to hold steady where I can, and when I fail, to accept that failure without turning away. Sometimes resilience leads us not to take the project or path in which we know we will succeed, but the one for which we know we are not ready, where we are not enough for the task, and where failure is the most likely outcome. In art and in life, at times, our greatest achievement is our most extravagant but honest failure.

In my life and work, resilience has been shaped by my family's history, by uncertainty, by exile, and by the necessity of reinvention. It has meant finding direction without assurances and moving through doubt without losing conviction. There have been moments when my resilience was tested—sometimes by dramatic situations, but more often by the quieter, more insidious forces of disillusionment, exhaustion, and the temptation to retreat. Yet each time, the question was not simply whether to persist, but how to do so without losing what mattered most. I have learned, sometimes against my assumptions, that resilience is not about hardening against the world but staying porous to it, allowing experiences to shape and reshape me without losing the thread of what I believe. Exile taught me this early. The severing from home, from language, from the familiar, was not something to overcome but something to live within. It was a condition that demanded adaptation, but also a refusal to be defined by loss.

The same is true in art. The work is full of thresholds—moments of doubt, of fear, of temptation to surrender one's integrity, of collapse, of needing to begin again. Resilience has meant staying with the work even when it turns against me, when what once felt certain can no longer be relied on. It has meant resisting the easy resolutions that would make things simpler but less true, resolutions that are a daily temptation in an art studio.

Artmaking can be difficult and humbling when one is working at the edge of what is possible, familiar, or understandable. At this edge, there are few assurances, and temporary failures are a guaranteed part of the process. These are not failures or calamities like those my parents faced or that many people endure regularly. Yet they can, and often do, wound the spirit and coax us toward the easiest or fastest way out. If these temporary failures wound the spirit, it is the repeated choice of these easy or fast escapes from the struggle of creating or living that confines and, ultimately, sickens the spirit.

Art depends on spirit and, like the sentinel metaphor of the canary in the mine, reveals the state of our spirit. Art is not a thing but an experience. While there are many ways to describe the nature of that experience, the way I find most telling, though admittedly less graspable, is that the experience brought about by a great work of art is a new emergent spirit arising from the interaction between the spirit the artist has instilled in the artwork and the spirit of the one engaging with it. Resilience is present on both sides of this exchange. It is not a fixed asset, not some gold of the heart, but a practice, one that involves more than strength or persistence. It requires the willingness to keep looking, to keep asking, to endure uncertainty without retreating into cynicism or false assurances. It is the discipline of continuing, but only in ways that remain honest.

When I faced periods of disillusionment in my career, resilience was not about pushing forward blindly but about questioning, reassessing, and finding my way back to what had initially had summoned me to be an artist. At critical moments, resilience has meant removing my armor, laying down my weapons, and, most difficult of all, dismantling the tower of myself I had built, and starting again with means that were less formidable but more honest—stronger not in force, but in their ability to sustain the long engagement that life requires.

I owe much to my parents, not only for their sacrifices, but for what they showed me about endurance.

Their example was imperfect, as all examples are, shaped as much by necessity as by will, by circumstance as by choice. If resilience is, as I have come to believe, a practice rather than a fixed trait, then I am still learning what it means, testing my understanding of it against the realities of life and work. There are times when I mistake persistence for resilience, when I hold on too long or let go too soon. I do not always recognize, in the moment, what is needed. But I return to the effort, not seeking certainty but clarity, often guided by art and writing, and by a commitment to what is honest and sustaining.

JH: First of all, why should we think we are not equipped for the long haul, for adaptation, and survival, the same resilient energy that supported our ancestors? Many, if not most of them, worked under far harsher conditions than most of us. Some of mine worked in mines, on farms, in factories, and those are the ones of whom I have some knowledge. They worked to survive; they worked without hope for something better; they sometimes fought in lethal wars, bore children, and suffered illnesses without modern palliative medicines and surgeries. Most of them lacked education, harbored no expectation of privilege, and had little to no sense of entitlement to anything better. I grew up with this legacy. How my life opened to opportunity was in part thanks to their sacrifices, luck, the help of some truly kind people along the way, and, I must surmise, the recondite blessing of some of the gods who run the universe. I did not merit these blessings any more than any of them, but they sometimes came to me nonetheless.

I often feel guilt for the privileges I received from such people even as I know that there is no grounds for guilt, only responsibility to make something of it. There is no day I forget this gift, no day I forget them, all the way back into the faded lands of ancestral memory. From them, I learned the work ethic, I learned not to expect anything not earned, not to quit, and occasionally, I learned the importance of a quiet dignity in the face of defeat and deprivation.

Of course, none of us know we have resilience until we are forced to face something very difficult and work our way through it. True, many folks give up, cave in, and shut something down inside that is fighting for life through them. Many of us have so acted, or failed to act, when depressed, marginalized by others, isolated, and flushed with self-doubt.

When I ask myself what has fueled my resilience, I see at least three sources: shame, a reason to pull through, and a fierce need to find the meaning in something. Let me look at them in this order.

First, the familial history I cited in the paragraphs above played a large role. As a result of lack of education, lack of mentors, and lack of opportunity, my family grew up in a world of shame, with a systemic sense of unworthiness, inadequacy, and incapacity. There are two sources of shame: a). having failed to meet some level of expectation, however misguided it might be, and/or b). feeling contaminated by the circumstances of one's life, the cultural milieu into which one was thrust by fate, and the stunted imagination of the possible that limits one's horizon. If we ask why a child's soul might feel shamed because of alcoholism, poverty, abuse, racism, sexism and other environmental messages, the answer is: because it is. Period.

My family's ethic of survival was to circle the wagons, take care of each other, and not to go "out there" unless forced to do so. During my last conversation with my mother, while she was dying of cancer, I told her of a book of mine being published in Sweden, the land of her father, thinking she would be pleased. She was appalled that I had published that book because it now meant her son was exposed to possible cross-fire from more entitled others. It would not have been understood by her that her son had gained some capacity to handle criticism, nor that he had to follow his own North Star. So it remains that my last time with her was swamped by the familiar fear and shame. To this day, such a memory of so many of whom I remain mindful, is a bugle call summoning the resilience to step into life, to go "out there," and to risk all in service to what wishes to be expressed through us.

Now I can more readily see how shame governed large areas of my life, producing avoidance of the task sometimes, or deliberately bad choices which befitted my deficient sense of inherent value. If shame is the lens through which one sees the world, one either confirms it daily, or one compensates. When you see a person flaunting wealth, acting as if they are better than anyone else, perhaps naming buildings after themselves, perhaps painting them gold, you are looking at a desolate inner life. Such a person is a psychological slumlord. The Swedish poet Tomas Tranströmer once wrote a poem in which the speaker is being shown about a city he is visiting. The tour, focused on the modern skyscrapers and malls, is meant to impress him. At the end of the tour, he says to his host that he is impressed but must wonder in the face of this flaunting of wealth if the slums must not then be inside of them.

Of the many arenas in which that pervasive sense of shame showed up, I will only cite one here. When, nearly three decades ago, I wrote a book titled *Swamplands of the Soul*, an examination of anxiety, depression, loss, guilt, addiction and other dismal denizens of the deep, I thought I had pretty much covered the waterfront. Yet the first person who read it outside the publisher said, “But you didn’t put shame in there.” And so I hadn’t. I was mortified, and privately, shamed. I neglected to address the one miasmic place that had played the greatest shadow role in my life. Surprise! Since that time, I have made a concerted effort, including here, to address the role of shame.

But having mentioned choices or conflicts avoided, I have not yet identified the compelling role shame played in my life. Shame showed up in me via a seeming virtue: resilience. I was, from mid-life onward, determined not to be defeated, not to quit, not to sabotage the possibilities. Since shamedom was such a dismal, awful place, I vowed not to go back there. And yet, as we know, what is denied within, shows up in subtle ways in our lives nonetheless. A lot of that resilience was fueled by the terror of shame. What is so critical in what we believe or what we do is not so much what we believed or did, but what that was in service to inside us. As the legal metaphor puts it, fruit from a rotten tree is still rotten. What appeared to be a virtue, and produced a few achievements here and there, was fueled by shame, not joy, not natural energy, but the flight from the awful.

Secondly, over the last few years I elected replacement of another knee, another hip, and having profited from both, being more mobile as it were, two cancers arrived. After multiple radiations, chemotherapies, and surgeries, my spine began disintegrating. The pain was extreme. Once, lying in bed, my body frozen with the rictus of contracture, I tried to walk, fell, and damaged the new hip. A kindly EMT lifted me onto a gurney and ferried me to the hospital. After two surgeries on the spine, I found myself in that twilight zone of pain-killers, rehab, trying to walk again, and wanting to die to end the misery. During this time, my wife, dealing with her own limitations, came to see me almost every day. Her image rising out of that mist stirred me to struggle anew, and to vow to come home, walk again, and be there for her. Dying, or giving up, seemed a betrayal of our relationship. This is one of the sources of my resilience, knowing that one has something of inestimable value for which to fight.

For many months, I wept in the morning, not only from the pain, but for the endlessness of it. But she was there for me; how could I not be there for her? Today, I walk a mile a day, although when I rise, it is not clear if the wires holding me together are going to hold another twenty-four hours. But, we have launched this project called a marriage, and I am resolved to do what I can. Sometimes, the best one can get from anger, or depression, or abuse is to resolve to carry on, as best one can. That kind of resilience, I am certain, allows certain abandoned mothers to rise each day and go off to demeaning jobs to take care of their children as best they can. No one is there for them, but they get up each morning. I love them for that. And for some men, the quiet dignity of labor, responsible labor, cleaning the bathrooms of others, digging the ditches, washing the dishes at the spa, is their resilience. It's all they have, but it is a glory that the privileged will never know. To maintain that dignity in undignified circumstances is a glory. Sometimes having a goal is all it takes to fuel the resolve to continue, and that we call resilience.

The third source of resilience which has supported me, even during the bad times, is the irresistible search for meaning. As discussed in the last chapter, meaning is not something we create, though the need for it is what keeps us going. As Jung once said, the smallest of things with meaning is always greater than the largest of things without meaning.

While I would not have used these words to describe my experience as a child, I recall wondering why my parents had to work so hard and never felt ownership of their lives, why my best friend, a black child named Kent across the street, was not welcome everywhere, why so many people were suffering during the terrible war that sucked up the oxygen during my first years. I remember feeling clearly, though not in these words, that I had to find out "why," what it all meant, and what I could do about it. In short, even as a child I thought: there has to be a meaning. I just don't know what it is. But I had to find out.

I know a lot more now, but I am still looking for the answers to those questions that swirled around me then. While I have learned to live without the answers to my questions, I am still on the hunt. For many years it took the form of education. If only I could read the right book, find the right teacher, I would get what satisfied the questing spirit. Assiduously, I studied the world religions and rich mythologies, and queried their prophets. These pursuits were inordinately valuable, and I still treasure them. But in the end, I concluded that the best I could do is be a teacher and pass on what little I knew, a therapist and be present to the struggles of another human being, and a writer to broaden the classroom whereby we might share the conversation and at least feel less estranged, less alone in our loneliness.

To this day, the old haunts of shame, the loving link to fellow sojourners, and the need to find meaning in all the suffering in the world, fuel me. A couple of years ago, about to undergo a painful procedure, the nurse said to me, "Go to your happy place now." She meant well, and I loved her for it, but I said, "This *is* my happy place." And so it is still. As a child, and even as a young naïve adult, I imagined that I could figure it out, find a place of understanding it all. Like Archimedes, if I could find a nexus, the omphalos of the world axle, to place my lever, I could lift the weight of the cosmos itself. While many in our culture sincerely offer their points of view of such a central nexus, they don't work for me. Again, I aver, it is not what you believe; it is *why* you believe it that matters. Rather all I can offer in return, indeed, all that I offer to anyone, is what little I know, and a large amount of compassion for their suffering.

Resilience is the energy, the drive, the will, the support from the little people toiling about in the solar plexus, to keep showing up for the next day, keep asking the same old questions, and refusing to shut up, or sit down, or mind our own business. This is what matters to me, and I have, and we have, resilience as the capacity to bounce back and keep on keeping on.

6

In your view, what is the connection between suffering and insight? Are there experiences or realizations that emerged from hardship, reshaping your understanding of growth or purpose?

> The life of man is misery:
> he finds no resting place, no haven from calamity.
> But something other dearer than life
> the darkness hides and mist encompasses.
>
> Euripides

JH: As I recall, it was Aeschylus, two and a half millennia ago who wrote, "The gods have ordained one solemn decree: that it is through suffering alone we come to wisdom." I would not quarrel with that assessment of the human condition though I would like to question the word "alone," for we can also have insight through serendipitous discovery, curiosity, the sharing with others, and we learn from our teachers, dumb accident, and the inherent impulse to wonder. When Sir Edmund Hillary was asked why he and Tenzing Norgay first climbed Mount Everest, his response was so profoundly human: "Because it is there." Such a spirit sent our ancestors across the turbulent seas to unknown shores, sends us into outer space, or causes an artist to attempt a new angle on an old subject. But it remains true, some of our most compelling insights rise from suffering. Suffering, after all, gets our attention, obliges a focus of energy, and often demands a review of it later to figure out what happened and what we need to learn to cope better in future. (As Jung pointed out, behind the wound, the genius of the person may emerge).

Take trauma, for example. Life is inherently traumatic if we define trauma as incursive experience that brings more quanta of energy than consciousness can understand or process at the moment. It remains neurologically hard wired within us whether we recall the event or situation consciously. This is why traumatic events are so long-lasting, so perseverant.

But insight may rise from trauma, or what may come is a false reading, and therefore, a false message. When something traumatic occurs our survival mechanisms immediately try to make sense of the experience. What happened, what caused it, what is its "message," what does it incline me to do or not do in future? Much of this "storying" is reflexive in character, and perhaps unique to the individual or context. The traumatic event is the phenomenon, but the epiphenomenon is the "story" that rises from the experience. Given that we do not know the actual causal factors much of the time, a story is created at the moment and ratified by repetition. Accordingly, often our earliest stories define a good part of our life, those stories which convey to us whether the other in our life is safe or unsafe, may be approached or avoided, and of course our status or worth vis á vis the other which the story narrates to us. Imagine turning your life over to a child's interpretations in the present conduct of your adult life, but we all do that as our psychic space is dotted with primal stories generated in childhood. Thus, our current patterns of avoidance, or aggression, or accommodation gain a reflexive, institutional authority in our lives. Because that is the story the trauma engendered, it is tied to that time and place. Thus, any "insight" it occasions may very well be limiting one's responses to the capacities of the child. Hence, the "insight" would be false. From such provisional epiphenomenal stories our life patterns emerge, based on deceptive premises. Part of the work of psychoanalysis is the sorting through these stories, lifting them into greater awareness, and when needed, challenging them. (I cited such a story in the discussion of shame in my life which rose from internalizing the conditions of one's life as a provisional definition of one's journey in an earlier chapter.) And also, the pragmatic task is to discern what these stories make us do or keep us from doing.

Another task of analysis recognizes what our stories were at that time and place might have been accurate then, their extrapolation into the current stage of our journey is prejudicial and often undermines our interests. It is as if one seeks to use the same pair of eyeglasses throughout one's life without factoring in the many changes to our eyes that occur. Our stories are "fictions," constructs that are meant to be informative but may deny our resilient powers and bind us to a disabling history. Sorting through these stories and their constrictive "conclusions" is one way we step into a larger summons than the readings of the past. Our stories may be invisible but our behaviors, or our patterns, are visible, and they allow us to work backward to reengineer our lives.

What is rendered visible is something consciousness can alter and transcend. Earlier this day, I listened to a man recount the heavy, heavy cloud that hung over so much of his life, generated by the pathologies of his family of origin, and compounded by a fundamentalist religion that demeaned his aspirant soul and judged him for a healthy exploration of curiosity. I said it was as if he was forever walking down the street backwards, seeing his present capacities through the limitations imposed by the story of that traumatic history. That metaphor spoke to him, and likely will support his revisioning the arc of his life.

The arc of all our lives involves an ongoing attempt to make sense of things and stay out of harm's way. When, for example, one's map of the world, or philosophy of life, is contradicted in a major way, a crisis occurs. Most of us, generalizing from the quid pro quo of our families systems, presumed that if one behaves, tries to do the "right thing," and means well, then the universe will reciprocate. This fallacy is renewed in each generation despite the *locus classicus* for its refutation in the book of *Job* nearly three millennia ago. Job was the archetypal "good boy," even superintending the piety of others around him. So when a ton of woe falls on his head, his whole world view collapses.

Similarly, many parentify the universe, perhaps succumbing to an imago Dei as judgmental Father figure, or they look to others to define their realities and explain to them what it is all about. In both cases, this move is an evasion of the summons to grow up, be responsible for one's own philosophy of life, ethical beliefs and practices, and it sabotages the recovery of personal authority. When troubles come, as they will, these makeshift constructs do not fare well. In our lack of knowledge, our utter dependency, and our intimidation by the magnitude of the past, all of us viewed our place in the universe this way. Some folks never move beyond that and remain psychospiritually infantile. I say this not in judgment but in sympathy. But I also know that all of us, sooner or later, are accountable for growing up.

No matter how careful we are, no matter how prudent, sooner or later life takes us to swamplands of the soul, places where the unforeseen consequences of our choice, or the choices of others, or the inexplicable universe will take us to places of suffering, loss, and philosophical if not physical dismemberment. I often reflect on the message of Viktor Frankl who lost his freedom, his family, his dignity, and everything in the concentration camps. But, he reflected, one thing remains, namely, the power to choose one's attitude in the face of the intrusive other. The way in which I put it the book *Swamplands of the Soul* written in the early 1990s is this: each swampland also brings to us a task, the addressing of which moves us from victimage to active participation in our lives. The way in which I put it to myself, and to clients, these days is, "How now, in the face of this over which you have no control, are you to live your life?" It is a variant on Frankl's insight, and focuses on a proactive challenge to changed behaviors, attitudes, or beliefs. Talk is cheap. Those difficult hours can truly wrench the soul, but then, no one and nothing owns our soul unless we give it away. That sentence, that challenge, is meant to pull a person out of the swamp wherein our personal dignity may have been lost back to an accountability for the dignity of the soul.

In the decades since writing about the swamplands I joined, along with other parents, the world's worst club, and lost a child. The world has continued in its awful bloody way with its strutting politicians, mass slaughters, gratuitous butchery, repeated injustices, and harm to innocents everywhere. As I noted earlier in these chapters, I went through multiple surgeries and experienced years of excruciating pain, as are many suffering down the street in Suburban Hospital from where I write these words. I came finally, to an obvious place, but even now find it difficult to articulate. I came to accept the suffering. That is hardly an original insight, and circles us back to Aeschylus. My oxymoron for this attitude is "militant submission." I choose not to think of myself as a victim. Stuff happens, and has always happened. Why should I think myself exempt? Why should I not see that it is now my turn, not someone else's? What arrogance would persuade me otherwise? Such "submission" is not passive, not surrender, it is a vigorous choice of a free person who also exercises existential revolt, a person who maintains a psychological privacy, dignity, and freedom in the context of an utterly contingent life.

While each of our lives is obviously unique, we are all the same in that we have to figure all this out for ourselves. The answers other folks offer, whether in good faith or charlantry, is *their* answer and not necessarily ours. And whatever the source, those answers may truly fail us when the push comes. Through the years, most folks had a larger story, a mythos that linked them to the four mystery realms of our lives: the cosmos, nature and its rhythms, supportive tribal rites and dogmas, and a personal psycho-philosophy that locates our tiny stories in a larger narrative. Whatever their conscious profession of belief today, more and more people have traded in the larger story for the inflation of ego consciousness and its delusion of power. This tradeoff means an increasing identification with the ego and its powers. And as we know, our ego attitudes can only fill the great vacancy partially. Even the person who affirms the old time religion, whose sense of history is tied up with a Paleolithic narrative, will demand the latest medications, surgeries, and life extension when the gurney brings their body into the O.R. Suffering may not bring insight but it will bring suffering.

"Militant submission" is the *anagnorisis*, the recognition that came to so many in the tragic sagas of the ancient world. So many of them had a sense of Kismet, fate, the implacable acts of the gods, and only a deluded fool would place oneself outside that field of energy. That is why the acceptance evidenced by the warrior who sings the death song before the killing can be so self-possessed. It is because he or she understands that they did not possess the self from the beginning. This concatenation of cells, governed and sustained by the continuity of the psyche, does not belong to us. That is only the ego blabbering away—a noisy, off-key tin horn player thinking it is the whole symphony.

And why should my puny, miserable little ego think it merits exemption from the great sweep of things? What delusional possession occurs to make it think it is special, or in charge, or exempt? Gautama the Buddha, whose generic name means "one who saw," so many years ago recognized that it is our understandable attachment to the ego state, and its fantasy of sovereignty, that most gets us into trouble. In the end, we are not in control. I think Buddhism was not meant to be a religion. It was a psycho-philosophy of life to address existential anxiety and to lead one to the modest conduct of a modest life—a considered life no longer entrapped in the delusion of perpetuity or enslaved to the anxiety of extinction.

So, "militant submission" means that I militantly, that is, with active participation and free will, submit to the larger order of things, the nature of which lies beyond my comprehension. I was not asked for my vote in these matters. The fact that I am mortal, finite, is not a problem for nature or the elusive divinities; it is only a problem for the nervous egos attached to the fantasy of their magnitude, the arrogance of the flea on the tossing mane of the lion. Suffering does sometimes bring insight, and insight repositions our relationship to all that lies about us. The ego state may not be thrilled with that insight, or may be threatened by it, but that is the problem for the ego. As Robert Frost so succinctly summarized in his poetic couplet, *The Secret Sits*:

We dance round in a ring and suppose,
But the Secret sits in the middle and knows.

EMC: Suffering often feels as if the world has singled us out for a special kind of punishment. In its immediacy, it is real and often overwhelming. Yet when examined more closely, much of what deepens our suffering arises not from pain itself but from the mind's insistence that life should be otherwise, that there exists some ideal version of events our lives have failed to meet. Pain is unavoidable. But suffering grows when pain becomes entangled with resistance, self-pity, or judgment. When we look inward with even a little distance, the "me" who suffers begins to lose solidity, and what remains is pain itself—sharp, undeniable, but freed from the narratives that magnify it. Seen in this way, suffering becomes both real and revealing: a mirror reflecting our illusions and attachments, and sometimes, when the reflection clears, a source of insight.

This clarity is difficult to convey. Although it doesn't stop many writers that it probably should, it's difficult to write about suffering without coming across as either distant or sentimental. The challenge lies in holding both its immediacy and its insight without diminishing either. Suffering is more prevalent and enduring than happiness, yet when it is our own and we try to draw meaning from it, the effort can easily slip toward self-indulgence or justification. Take, for instance, the suffering Oscar Wilde describes in his letter-book *De Profundis*. It is deeply personal, written during his imprisonment for "gross indecency" and the devastating losses and shame it brought to him and his family. In the letter, he sees his suffering as transformative, a crucible for refining the soul. While moving in its beauty and a sign of resilience, it risks aestheticizing suffering, a perspective that might diminish its weight. There's also the question of whether Wilde's view imposes a redemptive arc onto suffering, one that doesn't fit the experiences of those whose pain leads nowhere.

One whose pain led nowhere was Wilde himself. When he was released from prison, the transformation and growth he described in *De Profundis* did not translate into a resurgence in his personal or professional life. He left prison broken—physically, emotionally, and financially, and spent his remaining years in exile in France under a different name. His relationship with his family after his release from prison never fully recovered. His wife distanced herself from him following his conviction, and changed her surname and that of their two sons to avoid public association with Wilde. His health had deteriorated severely due to the harsh conditions of imprisonment, and he struggled with poverty and estrangement from society.

But despite these dangers and the distortions we almost always impose on our suffering, I find it valuable to consider the relationship between suffering and insight. This relationship has been explored and revealed in fairy tales, myths and religion. Christianity, a framework that has shaped the West's moral, cultural, intellectual, and political landscapes, has long taught that suffering and insight are intricately connected, a bond rooted in its deepest theological traditions and narratives, and understanding of the human condition, woven into the life of Christ himself. Through his passion and crucifixion, Jesus embodied the transformative potential of suffering, offering a framework that allows pain and struggle to transcend despair and become sources of revelation and growth. This connection is not limited to the example of Christ. It extends to the faithful. Saints like Teresa of Ávila and John of the Cross have described how trials and pain can strip away illusions and attachments, leading to a clearer vision of truth and a closer relationship with God. John of the Cross, in particular, speaks of the "dark night of the soul" as a profound spiritual experience where the absence of consolation and light paves the way for deeper insight and union with the divine. In this way, suffering is not seen as an arbitrary punishment or a meaningless burden but as a profound, though often painful, teacher.

Suffering disrupts the illusions of control, stability, and understanding upon which we rely. It shakes us and forces us to confront what we've ignored. Stripped of comfort and certainty, we're left exposed, and in that exposure, something shifts, or at least creates the possibility of shifting. Pain clears a space, sharpens the mind, and opens the heart. Through suffering, empathy deepens. Vulnerability makes us see others more clearly and binds us to them in ways that often surprise us. This became clear to me some years ago. I was facing some obstacles, and a friend suggested I go with him to a men's

Alcoholics Anonymous meeting. I decided to accept his invitation, even though I had never drank or taken drugs. I sat quietly to the side, listening as man after man spoke about their pain and their losses. The longer I listened, the more I felt like one of them. As a young guy, I had tended to see other men as rivals, but as I have gotten older, and especially that night, I recognized myself in the other men and them in me. We were all sailors, with much in common and in the same boat.

It has always been the case that we are more attuned to our own suffering than to the suffering of others. We feel our own suffering most sharply because it is close, because we live with it, because it shapes our days in ways no one else can fully see. The suffering of others exists at a distance. We might recognize it, sympathize, and sometimes grieve for it, but it does not press against us in the night or change the way we move through a room, unless we deeply love the sufferer. And so, we tend to measure pain unevenly, mistaking what is near for what is most significant, forgetting that what feels singular to us is, in truth, common to many.

In the arts, there is a tendency to see obstacles not as something most artists encounter but as a trial unique to ourselves. Our situation strikes us as especially unfair, and the opportunities that come our way particularly meager. While we know intellectually that this is not the case, our hearts feel the world's indifference as if we alone suffer it—or suffer it more deeply, more unjustly. It is not productive to measure or compare suffering. I have never known how to quantify my suffering. Have

I suffered much, or has my life been easy? When I share some aspects of my life, I gather a great deal of sympathy, and in those moments, I think that I have had my share of suffering. But at other times, when faced with great traumas, unthinkable losses, and unbearable conditions endured by others, I feel as though I have coasted through life, and it is in those moments that I am most cautious about speaking of my suffering.

Regardless of how significant or small my suffering has been, it has shaped the way I see the world and myself. For one thing, it has convinced me of the merit of humility, which is more surprising than it might seem. Growing up as an immigrant, facing challenging conditions, and living in a liminal space of neither here nor there tends to generate projections and ambitions that, despite having their roots in insecurity and inadequacy, can drive one forward.

Let me now return to the question of how I perceive the connection between suffering and insight. The Spanish poet Federico García Lorca ends his poem *Gacela of the Dark Death* with the lines:

> Because I want to sleep the sleep of the apples,
> and learn a mournful song that will clean all earth away from me,
> because I want to live with that shadowy child
> who longed to cut his heart open far out at sea.

Like Lorca, I see suffering as having the power to cleanse and strip away what is unnecessary. It could wash away illusions and expose what we have hidden even from ourselves. In suffering, we are laid bare, usually not as we wish to see ourselves, but as we are, with our frailties, attachments, and mistaken certainties. Suffering, if confronted honestly, can dissolve—at least temporarily—the trivial concerns that once seemed pressing and bring into focus what cannot be ignored: what we love and what we fear.

We don't always face suffering honestly. It is not unusual to resist what it reveals. Confronted with pain, we sometimes respond by torturing ourselves with the belief that we deserve better while fearing we have brought it upon ourselves. Or we search for someone to blame, as if pinning our suffering on another might make it easier to bear. Or we find a theory that intellectually packages it away from our hearts. Suppressed or ignored, suffering has a way, like a roof leak, of appearing where we least expect it, often in forms that are more damaging and more difficult to address. Pain that is left unattended seeps into our choices, relationships, and work, sometimes disguising itself as cynicism, detachment, or ambition. These reactions are natural, but they keep us trapped in a smaller, more self-enclosed understanding of suffering.

Resistance is not the only way we misuse suffering. Even when we acknowledge it, there is the danger of becoming consumed by it rather than transformed through it. It's not always easy to find a balance between recognizing what we have endured and allowing it to define us. The arc from self-concern and blame to a broader recognition of suffering is neither simple nor comforting. It does not erase pain or always bring peace, but it shifts its weight, making it something we endure not as isolated individuals but as an intrinsic aspect of what it means to be human.

Once we develop an honest and open relationship with suffering, we then can work in how we respond to it, whether we use it to deepen our understanding, to move forward with greater awareness, to practice our patience and gratitude, or whether we allow it to harden us, to make us smaller, more inward, more consumed by our own pain. Suffering has helped me see my choices and values more clearly. The most difficult periods of my life have shown me how much of what I once considered important, both in myself and my work, was of little real significance. Suffering stripped away some of my illusions about myself, my ambitions, the points of view I carried from my upbringing, and the narratives I constructed to make sense of the world. It dismantled distractions I once clung to and exposed what remained when comfort, certainty, and external validation fell away.

In its most brutal form, suffering leaves little room for pretense. It forces an honest reckoning with what we value, what we can live without, and what endures. This kind of clarity can reveal the shallowness of desires and the hollowness of what once seemed important. But there is also relief in it, shedding excess, and recognizing that much of what we spend our lives chasing is trivial in the face of real hardship.

Even so, how we deal with suffering rarely unfolds in neat, disciplined ways. There are times when the way out of some hellish hole is raw, embarrassing, even destructive. I used to feel ashamed of my own episodes of melodrama or confusion, but as I have learned to face suffering with more steadiness, I have also grown less judgmental of those moments. Perhaps I am more aware now of how close any of us are to being undone. One tragedy, one catastrophe, and we are stripped of whatever dignity we thought we had. Perhaps the way I am most indebted to suffering is in its appearance and reappearance in my life as a force that challenges what I might have thought my purpose was, or, more accurately, my many purposes, a plurality that is true for most of us. In my role as a father, for instance, suffering has kept me up many nights, forcing me to reconsider my purpose and the balance between what we can and cannot control. Whatever assumptions I had about knowing how to raise a child have been broken and mended by the suffering that, along with beauty and many happy moments, accompanies parenting. As an artist, suffering has brought me face to face with my limitations and has tested my resolve. It is that testing of my resolve that has most clarified my understanding of purpose, partly by subjecting my energies, directions, reasons, and visions to the purifying fire of anguish and doubt. I owe much of what I understand about resilience, love, forgiveness, and compassion to suffering. Without it, I would be a more trivial and less loving person, and a shallower artist, if an artist at all.

Creativity and Engagement with the World

7

What is creativity, and what is the process by which you bring into the world what you do?

When I write, I do not make big plans,
I have the text inside of me.

Werner Herzog

EMC: Creativity resists description and instruction. Every attempt to explain or teach it runs into the same obstacle: the essential element in the creative act cannot be prescribed or formulated. Part of what gives art its power is the mysterious depth from which something unexpected emerges. When I walk into my studio in the mornings, I am usually concerned with the question: What is art, and how do I bring it about? It doesn't appear inside me as words but as the desire for a mute painting to hum, or the insistence of an embryonic work wanting to be brought to life. In the studio, this question takes as many forms as there are paintings, drawings, and sculptures, yet at its core it is a question of creativity—not as problem solving but as attunement to something larger than myself. And if creativity is not problem-solving, what happens when we begin to see life as a problem to be solved?

The Greek King Sisyphus approached every challenge as a problem, even death. When it came for him, he tricked and bound it, temporarily avoiding his fate. This was as creative as it was futile, for none of us can outmaneuver death. By focusing so narrowly on evading the immediate situation, he failed to grasp that death is not a problem to solve but an inherent part of life, and he paid a price for this shortsightedness: an eternity of pushing a boulder uphill only for it to roll back down. In treating mortality as a puzzle to fix, he missed the chance to understand his place in a greater relational whole and, perhaps, to find meaning in his transience.

Every situation, even a favorable one, can be framed as a problem, and once we do, the context shrinks and our focus narrows to finding the solution. Yet every situation, including death, holds its own universe of conditions and possibilities. Across traditions, death is seen not as an end but as a passage: the Greeks imagined the honored dead in the Elysian Fields, Hindu thought folds death into an unbroken cycle of rebirth, and *The Tibetan Book of the Dead* envisions it as a threshold where perception expands beyond the illusions of self. Even in Christian monasteries, windows are set to face cemeteries, so that the rhythm of daily life unfolds against a constant awareness of transience. Such practices echo Heidegger's claim that only by fully confronting death do we come to an authentic relationship with life. At the bed of death, he writes, all distractions fall away, leaving only the essence of existence. In recognizing our finitude, we are freed from the inauthentic pull of convention, and death, when faced, does not diminish life but enlarges it.

Philosophers, too, have resisted the impulse to see death as a failure. Seneca advised familiarity with death, not avoidance, writing, "He who has learned how to die has unlearned how to be a slave." When ordered by Nero to take his own life, he accepted it, even when it became miserable and drawn out. For him, the awareness of death was not a burden but a liberation that freed him from the fear that keeps us from fully living. *The Hagakure*, by Yamamoto Tsunetomo, says that "The Way of the Samurai is found in death." In medieval *vanitas* paintings, death is not just an intrusion but a counterpoint, a reminder that beauty and decay are intertwined. In the poetry of Hölderlin and the paintings of Rothko, death presses against life, deepening it rather than negating it.

Sisyphus, however, failed to see death in any of these revelatory ways. He saw it only as an obstacle, a final problem to overcome, and in doing so, he reduced it to something to be evaded, delayed, tricked. His ingenuity allowed him to escape for a moment, but it was an escape into a narrower, smaller existence, not a greater one. His defiance, though clever, was ultimately unimaginative. His creativity, bound by its own limited view of what mattered, led not to greater freedom but to an eternity of repetition.

Creativity, when reduced to problem-solving, risks becoming an exercise in control, a reflexive attempt to master uncertainty. The expression attributed to Maslow, "If all you have is a hammer, everything looks like a nail," reminds us that when creativity is reduced to cleverness or ingenuity, it narrows rather than expands our way of seeing, turning the world into a series of obstacles to overcome rather than an expansive reality to engage with. How we see and attend determines the reality available to us: attention can be narrow and goal-oriented or open, receptive, and capable of perceiving complexity. If we move through the world always looking for problems to solve, we may succeed in imposing order or impressing others with our flair, but often at the cost of deeper understanding.

Philosophers and artists have long resisted this instrumental view of creativity. Heidegger spoke of *Gelassenheit*—a letting be—suggesting that true understanding does not come from imposing order but from dwelling within the complexity of existence. Rilke urged openness rather than resolution, writing in *Letters to a Young Poet*: "Be patient toward all that is unsolved in your heart and try to love the questions themselves." Creativity, in this sense, is not about solving but about enlarging, deepening our relationship with experience rather than forcing it into something graspable.

This broader creativity seeks neither control nor surprise. It is an act of attunement, a willingness to be shaped by what one encounters. The works of art, literature, and philosophy that move me tend to arise not from mastery over a subject, but from surrender to it. Sisyphus, had he understood his fate differently, not as a curse but as a condition of being, might have arrived at a meaning beyond problem-solving, beyond escape.

To see differently is not just to think differently but to be differently. A wider attention shifts not only what we notice but how we inhabit the world. Frequently, the reason artists cannot make deeper work is not because of their skills or knowledge, but because of who they are. Where problem-solving seeks to take hold of something, open, receptive attention allows something to unfold. It is not a passive drifting or an overpowering, but an active participation in the unfolding of reality, where meaning is not imposed but revealed. Creativity, approached this way, is not about force or cleverness but about the ability to see what is actually there rather than what we expect or wish to find.

This is easier said than done. Few of us like uncertainty, and when confronted with something ambiguous or challenging, we instinctively try to contain it by framing it as a problem to be solved. We tend to favor methods and techniques that promise clarity, offering a way out of the maze or a solution to the puzzle. The impulse is understandable: problems have answers and solutions give us control, so it's not surprising that creativity is often seen less as an opening into the unknown than as a clever way to navigate existing systems.

The idea of a "creative culture" and the rise of "creatives" as an identity have popularized this view, becoming institutionalized in art schools, university curricula, and corporate recruitment strategies. This framing of creativity that rewards disruption, novelty, and marketable difference has become so dominant that I find it necessary to step back from it entirely in order to create space for something else.

The term "creatives" itself feels like a corporate abstraction, flattening the personal, nuanced, and varied processes of creativity into a marketable label. Rather than acknowledging the depth, struggle, and lived experience inherent in creative work, it emphasizes its most superficial traits—ingenuity, trendiness, aesthetic appeal. It is creativity repackaged as innovation, something sleek and efficient, stripped of its emotional and spiritual dimensions. This broad categorization oversimplifies what are necessarily diverse approaches, reducing creativity to an identity category, when in reality, it is an internal, transformative, and often messy process that cannot always be measured, commodified, or explained.

As far as I can tell, the most valued skill of corporate creatives is problem-solving. They connect disparate ideas, decide which elements to keep or discard, and bring about changes with imagination and insight, or with embellishments and surprises the culture favors and hails as new (though they are often derivative). When faced with an impasse, the best among them find one or several ways to resolve it with elegance and cleverness, leaving us to wonder, "How did you get from here to there?" or "Why didn't I think of that?"

I understand creativity to be something different. Perhaps it is because, as an artist and former scientist, my creative efforts aren't and weren't seeking wide approval. In the case of art, the main audience is me, along with the works, ideas, people, and influences I trust and admire. In science, for example, creativity leads to insights and discoveries that, for the most part, are impressive not when they are "creative" but when they are truthful.

Although I understand the impulse to think of creativity as problem-solving, I find that when I start thinking of situations as problems to solve, my attention shifts to calculation, and elements in the field of attention become obstacles or discrepancies between the current state and whatever goal is desired. There's something restrictive about seeing situations this way, and often, a price is paid for the consequent narrowing of attention.

For me, creativity is a way of bringing about a new state of being that responds not only to what first captured my attention but also to who I am, how I am changing in the process, and the workings of the world I can account for, while allowing space for what I sense but cannot fully articulate. The outcome of this creativity may not always appear "creative," in the sense it might be not be clever, fashionable, or practical.

As I see it, the goal of art, where creativity is central, is not to satisfy our appetite for the novel or the clever. It is to move us emotionally while offering clarity and a connection to all that is. This movement is deep and powerful, more like an inaudible rumble through our being than a trumpet blast with confetti. Yet much of what is said about creativity favors the latter.

Let me end with an example of how I approach creative work.

A few years ago, after a trip to St. Petersburg, Russia, I began working on a large painting inspired by a bridge I saw there. The first thing that appeared on the canvas was not the bridge but an apple tree, big and old, with twisted leaves and heavy fruit. Over time, the tree disappeared under layers of paint, replaced by the image of a stone-arched bridge seen up close, water running beneath it.

The painting took five years to complete. Not because of intricate details. It was a relatively simple form, mostly black, gray, and brown, with a few crude highlights marking the slow shift of water beneath the bridge. I painted in the sky in the upper right-hand corner, then painted it out—about a dozen times—the only part that suggested a world beyond the bridge. These changes were not about solving a compositional or thematic problem, but about searching for a way to unconceal the nature of painting and its relationship to the world. If there was a problem to solve, it was not the painting but myself: my limitations and my inability to see what was already there behind the clutter of expectations and assumptions.

There is a rumor that art-making is a consequence of the eye—the so-called good eye—and the hand. Others believe that to the eye and the hand one must add sophistication and knowledge of art. And that, for the most part, is what we consider the ingredients of creativity and the forces that bring about a work of art. But creative work in which those are the only considerations tends to be superficial and transitory. Those who can endure the contradictions it raises, and the ridicule from materialists and those who view art as a form of cultural production, insist that the heart must be involved in the bringing about the experience of art. The heart charges art with its power to move us, and that is good. But that is not where an art practice needs to end. In its deepest manifestation, art arises from a stillness within, from a deep awareness that has been called by many names. It is when this awareness enters and guides the process that art becomes resonant not only with emotion, the energy of the materials, and art's history, structure, and dynamics, but also with something fundamental and enduring in all that exists. As a shorthand, we can call this presence, and the process that brings it about is, in my view, creativity.

Creativity is not about surprising myself or others with an ingenious solution to the problem of a diagonal bridge on a flat canvas, and, judged by many of the assumptions we hear about creativity, the finished painting was unimpressive. The imagery was neither wild nor new, and it invoked no flourish or cleverness. That was how it had to be. The difficulty lay in recognizing and eliminating those intellectual and artistic tricks.

The truth of the painting depended on quieting those qualities, on stepping outside the need to impress or solve, so that Being could unfold from a deeper source, one reached when we are not distracted by frills.

JH: Reportedly, King George III of England once accosted Edward Gibbon, author of the 1776 *The Decline and Fall of the Roman Empir*e, and said to the scholar, "Another damn'd thick, square book! Always, scribble, scribble, scribble! Eh! Mr. Gibbon?" Never mind that the scholar had just spent five years of his life toiling to produce the second of the multi-volumed history. Similarly, the famed Dr. Johnson auto-described a lexicographer as "a harmless drudge." So many folks think of writing a book, whether it be poetry, or fiction, or history, as something like a hen dropping a daily egg—a strange operation peculiar to that species, and no more an interactive act than brushing one's teeth.

But starting still another book is like setting out in a sailing ship to an unknown world, not knowing if we will ever make it there. The ship leaks, and the timbers crack and groan.

Each departure is the last such voyage… At least till the next one.

It is scary but irresistible. Kierkegaard once observed that "merchant ships hug the coastline, but men-o-war open their orders out on the high seas." But it never ceases being scary. As the Naval Hymn has it, "O Lord, Thy ocean is so large, and our boats are so small."

But that is why we, sea and human, are placed in proximity with each other.

But what is creativity, and from whence it comes?

Is it intentional, and if so, why, despite our intentions does it so often fail to arrive? These are quiddities upon which humankind has speculated for many millennia. We know that we can generate a grocery list before we go to the store. We can write and pass bills in legislatures. We can write love letters, documents, instructions on how to find a location, and myriad other "scribblings."

Many believe that they have a great novel within them. If so, we do we so seldom see it? Perhaps the most ridiculous depiction of the labor of creation was portrayed in *Night and Day,* the 1946 Hollywood film of the life of Broadway composer Cole Porter. Played by Cary Grant, the musician is in a bombed out farmhouse in war-ravaged France. He yearns for inspiration like a love-sick hound. But wait! The rain is leaking through the tattered roof. Ah yes, "like the drip, drip, drop…" Then the old clock manages to produce a sound… "Like the tick, tick, tock of the stately clock as it stands against the wall." After several literal and labored interventions such as this, the distinguished Mr. Porter, stroking a concert piano that just happened to be part of this bucolic furniture, bursts into rhapsodic "Night and Day… You are the one. Only you beneath the moon and under the sun."

The description above is a literal account of a literal account of the creative process. As such it is ludicrous, but how then is a director to depict the creative act without falsifying it? Even ham-handed as this description is, the film is not the first to speculate that artist is guided by the literal and becomes a sort of divine amanuensis, or perhaps a divine ventriloquist. (Actually a fine work of literary analysis of the English Romantic poets by Edward Bostetter was titled *The Romantic Ventriloquists: Wordsworth, Coleridge, Keats, Shelley, Byron.* The metaphor obviously implies that the gods are speaking through the mouth of the poet, the poet then being a vehicle for the transcendent energies seeking incarnation on the terrestrial plane). But this notion of possession by the transcendent powers goes back further and shows up in the ancient concepts of the *Daimon* and the *Muse*. Our ancestors also observed that we can differentiate the variegated levels of consciousness at work in any given moment. We identify ourselves through the lens of consciousness but an infinite number of other energies are at work, monitoring the body, generating feeling reactions, pooling up as mood states, transforming into projections or convictions or framings of the moment. They knew from first-hand experience that some unconscious content could usurp any ego-state at almost any time. Jung's employment of the "complex," those clusters of psychic energy, helps explain why we might have made certain choices or why we were in an altered state. The German word he employed to describe this usurpation of the ego was *Ergriffenheit*, which translate as "possession." When we are in a powerful complex, our view of the world is altered. We may say, hyperbolically, that we are transiently psychotic, at least until the complex's energy plays out and falls back into the unconscious. Our classical ancestors might alternately say, "Mad Ares stormed him into fury," or "Sullen Aphrodite withdrew her powers and left them bereft." All of these depictions intuited the presence of "other" material, not apparently of the ego's intention or origin.

When, for example, Socrates accounts for his "inspiration," he attributes it to the tutelage of the Daimon. The Daimon is not a demon—though later religionists feared that they might be admitting evil spirits to their closed pantheon—but rather an intermediary spiritual presence, having an instructive, tutelary function. The Daimon bridges for us the vast expanse between the gods and human beings. Through the hermetic Daimones, the gods inform us, instruct us, frequently correct us. Similarly, the Muse, is drawn from classical link to "inspiration." Even John Milton, the classic Christian apologist, begins his baroque text by petitioning, "Of man's first disobedience, and the fruit of that forbidden tree, Sing, Heavenly Muse." So the Muse derives from the righteous pagans, but receives a comforting baptism with the assurance that its recondite source is still "heavenly." Similarly, the medieval thinker Ficino noted that many poets compose as if mad, not knowing what they said during that transported state, and they may have been used as an instrument of Divine will.

Both the Daimon and the Muse are personifications of an energy that lies outside of conscious control and, having visited, regrettably retains sufficient autonomy to depart whenever it wishes. We have all had such moments of "visitation." One could even say, when a complex is activated, a field of energy constellated, we experience an Other which may be wholly within, and dissociated, but it is experienced as Other. Many claim having experienced such phenomena as angels, or evil spirits, or even that chap in the red underwear and horns, the Devil. Dissociation occurs when a cluster of energy has sufficient power in its own right to encroach upon the ego state, or when triggered can produce a flashback, a sudden panic, an undermining of the ego's capacity to contain its boundaries. Think, for example, of our dreams, which sleep research tells us we all do, and continuously, though we may not remember them. Many of our antecedents believed such "travels" to be literal, or visitations of the gods, or, in the shamanic tradition, loss of soul. (Once in a post-operative state, filled with palliative pain medication, I was convinced two Mafiosi were at the foot of my bed and were trying to kill me. I arched my back up over the restraining braces in the bed and hit the tile floor on my cheekbone. Another time, I was convinced that my physician was the star of a musical titled, get this, *On the Development of Agriculture and Industry in Ohio in the Nineteenth Century*. (!) There he was with straw hat, bowtie, and cane, dancing and singing his heart out. I was so completely convinced that these psychic apparitions—and psychologically, they were real—had actually occurred that it took my wife and doctor combined to convince me I had hallucinated.)

We all seek inspiration at some moments in our lives, some infusion of energy that transforms our sensorium and reframes our experience. In seeking inspiration (*spirare*, "to breathe,)" we summon the breath of the gods to infuse us with a touch of divinity. Remember the old hymn, "Breathe in Me Breath of God," or Shelley's pagan rhapsodic "Ode to the West Wind."

My personal experience of writing is much closer to what painter Chuck Close concluded when he said amateurs wait for inspiration, while serious artists show up at the studio and get to work. Yes, there is such a thing as an artistic block. In early academia, I wrote the first book in America on the British playwright Harold Pinter, and then I did not write again for over twenty years. While I started several critical manuscripts, I came to realize something in me did not want to write to keep a job in academia. It violated my soul. When our last child went off to her adult journey, some twenty books emerged. Clearly, my inner world had an attitude about imposed "publish or perish" servitude, and waited until it was finally being respected.

I once knew a fine poet and psychoanalyst who specialized in resolving blocks in creative artists. That she had a background of singing in operas caused me to suspect that she had had many a wrestle with the noonday demon, or the black dog, as various folks have described. I cannot over-emphasize the fact that creative process is a gift, but it also has to be earned. Every book I have written has occurred at the end of a long day's work, after supper, or on a free part of a weekend, when someone else might turn on the telly, or go for a walk. Each one has been a product of a willingness to sacrifice some comfort, resist some distraction, to show up and wrestle with that self-doubt. Without that willingness, the work does not happen. As I frequently say to my whining self, "shut up, suit up, show up."

On the other hand—and there is always another hand—it is true that on more than one occasion, I awoke with a paragraph rolling out of my mind. More than once I got up in the middle of the night to type that transmission lest it slip away. From whence this source comes is, of course, the dynamic unconscious that never sleeps. If it did, we would die on the spot as our heart would stop. I have come now to personify that process as consulting "the little people" downstairs. When my brain is a loggerheads with some issue, whether creative or quotidian, I "put it down there" for the little people to work with. They always do, and they usually get back to me with their report, but not typed on my desk by five p.m. as I would wish. They arrive while driving, or in the middle of the night, or when I wish to be left alone. I recently wrote a colleague a declination of her invitation to write an essay for an anthology on the conflict between good and evil. I laid down to take an afternoon nap and woke to find the paragraphs rolling out. I immediately sent a second email to indicate I would undertake the challenge and she happened to read the second email before the first.

I truly believe this source of developmental dialogue exists within each of us. The "little people downstairs" are our intra-psychic components, and if we, over time, risk developing a conversation with them our sense of gravity will shift from outer to inner. I believe that each of us has a source of wisdom, the wisdom of nature that is soliciting our concurrence. As Emily Dickinson wrote in the 1860s, the sailor cannot see the North, but knows the needle can. Her metaphor suggests that we all need to find our inherent compass. Failing to do so leaves us at the mercy of whatever complex is activated within or the greatest pressure confronting us from without.

How that all occurs, I do not know, but it is a "flow" experience, and when I am in it it is as if I am possessed. It is not hard for me to understand why our ancestors called these moments visitations by the gods, the Daimones, the Muses. While it is true that fortune favors the prepared mind, when we are respectfully open to the intentionality of the unconscious, it is far more likely to manifest in some palpable images. It would be psychospiritually wrong for me to claim credit for those moments, but I do know that if I were not willing to sit down and open myself, brush back the attendant demons of doubt and intimidation, they would not visit. And who, then, would be the blame for that if they did not?

8

How do you perceive the relationship between solitude and creativity? Are there instances where solitude has clarified or intensified your vision?

There is a solitude of space
A solitude of sea
A solitude of death, but these
Society shall be
Compared with that profounder site
That polar privacy
A soul admitted to itself—
Finite infinity.

Emily Dickinson

JH: The traumatic loss of relationship brackets our short time on this planet. Floating through time and space—those constructs of later conscious life—all needs met, no bills to pay, no schedules to meet, the child is violently expelled from its home and thrown into life. (We are "thrown," *entworfen*, into existence, Heidegger says.) And somewhat later, after the last breath, one departs from all one has known. And in between, is the great loneliness. As the great modern philosopher Yul Brynner once observed, "We are born alone, live alone, die alone, and friends along the way are bonuses." As a child, I had many playmates, organized many a time and place to meet to play football, rode bikes to rendezvous, and yet, my best times were spent alone. I loved to climb a fence that allowed me to jump to our garage roof and from there my grade school self could see into the backyards of neighbors. For me, those little plots of land were foreign nations. I could see them but was forbidden to go there. My pubescent self similarly loved to climb trees and see over rooftops. Like Robert Frost, I was a swinger of birches. When the wind blew I was not risking life and limb, but was of course high in the rigging of a Yankee Clipper departing Cape Hatteras and perhaps from there bound to exotic Cathay.

But the world has its way with us. As Wordsworth noted back in his 1802 "Ode on Intimations of Immortality," we enter this temporal plane trailing clouds of glory but by late adolescence, early adulthood, it has faded into the light of common day. So many vacations are spent by the sea shore, or in the national forests, or mid the mountain ranges, for the ancestral memory of being in a larger frame of reference, linked again to our natural home, if not consciously then in our fever dreams and moments of reverie, perseverates within us.

However linked to others, we are all alone; no one else resides in our bodies, our emotional frames, or fully shares our complexes, our aspirations, our fears. So great is the threat of being alone, that I know many folks who are in terrible marriages, or geographies they hate, but they remain because of that existential terror. As one client said to me, "I won't let go of this hand in the darkness until another hand is there to grasp."

Ironically, for all our electronic connectivity, we are more and more atomized, more separated from each other. In my childhood people knew their neighbors, gathered in the evenings to share the news, went to the ballpark to watch a softball game and eat ice cream. Somewhere in the 1950s, as if a plague visited the land, the streets emptied. One walked down the street and saw a little bluish glow from the living room. Television had arrived and with it the demise of so much community.

Loneliness is now a national pathology. Some nations, such as Japan and the U.K., have cabinet level positions with combating loneliness as their portfolio. All addictions are reflexive anxiety management strategies. Probably rivaling only food pathologies, no addiction is more compelling than the internet that promises immediate connection. (Just try to separate teenagers from their cell phones and see what a ruckus is aroused.) No matter how many distractions, palliative measures, sooner or later, most people have to confront the reality that no one here is going to fix their lives for them, spare them surcease of anxiety, or keep them from their mortal appointments. The more we depend on the other the more we will fail to recognize the delusion of "togetherness" that Chekhov wryly skewered in his observation that if one was afraid of loneliness, one should not get married. Having done so, it is only a matter of time before one is obliged to recognize that the other will not and cannot take care of it all for us. In fact, we can have quality relationships with others and yet realize the more we are enmeshed with others, the less differentiated we are as a human being, and the less likely we are bringing our unique developmental selves into this world. This act, what Jung called "individuation," is both our summons and our gift to the world.

Individuation is not individualism, or narcissism, it is a willing submission to nature's imperative to become ourselves, the highest and most difficult of prospects.

And now, the good news. There is a "cure" for an addiction. It is the ability to face, to experience, perhaps to suffer that which the addiction is seeking to treat without the palliative behavior. In other words, one has to experience consciously what one has already been experiencing. And now, the cure for loneliness: it is solitude!

When one achieves solitude, one is not lonely while being alone. In his *Letters to A Young Poet*, Rilke beautifully points out that we are set down in life as our natural element, and are equipped with the wherewithal needed to survive and to prevail over our dependencies. While it is true that we are social animals, and need others for the dialectic which enlarges us, we are also granted by nature the resilience, the insight, and the summons to live the journey. What nature does not give us is courage for the long haul. We have to find that within ourselves the hard way.

At various times in my life I suffered intense loneliness. During long stretches throughout my retraining as an analyst in Zürich, away from family and friends, and limited in budget, I rode the trams for entertainment. If the weather was good, I went to the ubiquitous parks or walked beside the lovely Zürichsee. If the weather was foul, as it usually was in the winter, I rode those trams and memorized their many tram stops. Fourteen lines, with at least ten stops per line, meant a lot to remember but it was partly how I made my limitations interesting. What I most learned during that time was that I could survive being alone, and that what it forced me to do is develop the conversation within, which got richer and richer. Part of that richness rose from the insights of personal analysis, working with dreams and the techniques of active imagination. And part of it rose from talking to myself and listening to what came up for me. I do not wish to romanticize this experience; it was an ordeal, but also a powerful and transforming relationship to the unconscious.

Years later, while attending a professional meeting in Birmingham, Alabama, I went to visit the city art museum. Later, walking through the streets, I felt a wave of anxiety inexplicably wash over me. What was that, I asked myself? It was a pleasant afternoon with a survey of some new art in a new city. And then it came back to me. The mere analogy of being on my own in a strange city brought back the isolation and the loneliness of that Zürich experience. The difference was, this time I had the strength and the technique of querying myself to get to the root of that disturbing affect. I had learned to go into it, not run from it, to name the formless and shapeless, and realize that I had the core strength to bear it, to trust what was being experienced without the palliative distraction. That is the gift solitude can and does bring the lonely. After decades together, my wife and I have often discussed how we will be after the death of one or the other. It will be devastating; it will be awful. And we both are clear that the survivor will survive, and will go on with the business of living. We will honor our relationship by remembering, valuing, and serving the values that brought us together, and energized our joint but separate transits.

Having had an early life in academia, I spent so much of my time, as we were trained to do, looking around for corroborative evidence, or anticipating contradictory evidence. That is the gift of academia, not falling into the conclusion of one's preference, but sorting through the range of data and finding the most defensible posture from among the many possible. This evaluative process serves the search for the most compelling truth very well. It also makes one nervously look around for consensual agreement, not unlike a child wishing the support of peers. Shortly after academia, my first writing was spent with the felt belief that academic colleagues were looking over my shoulder, waiting to pounce on an unsupported generalization, if not, horrors, a misstatement of fact. Today I do almost no research for my books. I don't take that position out of any arrogant inflation, but rather a desire to explore what I have seen, felt, concluded on my own. In academia, too many people are present; in a mature person writing, perhaps too few exist: one is enough. But alone one tasks oneself with the challenge to sort through the problem on one's own, to find the position that most describes one's personal discoveries, and to take that risk. Given my upbringing, described in an earlier chapter, such a risk is very much out on the periphery of the acceptable. It certainly does not lend itself to validation or support. But what I have found is that if one expresses as sincerely as possible what one has experienced and concluded, it will touch other people. And if it is unknown to them, it will encourage them to step into that mist-laced borderland and explore for themselves.

Today solitude is essential for creative work, whether exploring dreams, reflecting on cases, wondering about a snag in a relationship, or opening the door to insight through writing. While one employs ego consciousness to bring matters to the surface, I find that the work has already been going on below in the realm of the unconscious. Just as divorces occur inwardly long before they become a conscious decision, and just as loss is processed inwardly long before one sorts through it all consciously, so we may say that the creative process is an essential aspect of our functioning. We do not make up those dreams, those intrusive thoughts at three a.m., those sudden insights into what is really going on. The psyche is already at work in all of us. It is my reflection on this intra-psychic activity that persuades me that we are not alone when we are alone. It is those moments of awareness of the goodly conversation going on within that brings us the gift of solitude.

Nothing I am suggesting here is meant to devalue the importance of relationship. I would not be writing this book without the gift of a relationship with Enrique. His motive, I am sure, is to grow by engaging me with compelling questions, and it certainly is my motive in agreeing to participate. As I argued in *The Eden Project*, a study of relational dynamics, the gift of the other is their "otherness." Their otherness allows, demands perhaps, that we grow through internalizing and containing that otherness and witnessing our enlargement through this engagement. The more infantilized the relationship, the more we expect the other to replicate our views and values, and support our shaky hold on things. Only tolerating the otherness of the other is not enough for that may simply be a co-dependent variant. Growing from the otherness of the other is what gets us an education.

In homeopathy, one ingests a bit of the toxin to inure oneself to the pathogenic agent. Embracing one's aloneness is the best preparation for enduring loneliness, but also for improving the quality of our relationship to the other. Jung pointed out that none of this recognition is sociophobia, or protective avoidance; quite the contrary, it is the alone person who is most sensitive to the nuances and canyons of relationship. Another way of looking at all this is: the more I can tolerate myself, the more able am I to not only tolerate the other, but be less enmeshed with the other in a regressive fusion. The less I am dependent upon the other to define my experience, the more I am obliged to access, and in time to trust, the autonomous process going on within. This is, again, not an endorsement of narcissism, or solipsism; it is a humbling recognition that something deep within each of us knows what is right for us and it is trying to get through to us through the feeling function, the energy systems, the dreams, and when ignored, through our symptoms. The deepest definition of relationship I know comes from Rilke again, where he suggests that our task is to be the caretaker of another person's solitude. Each person brings his or her aloneness to the meeting, and from that, the alchemy of enlargement can occur. Two plus two equals five. When that happens, we feel more at home in the world, but we can't get there without accepting our solitude in the first place. After all, the flight from solitude is the flight from oneself. And if we are fugitives, how could we ever be there in an authentic way with another?

Recently I received a letter from a man in his thirties who wrote from Greece that he was heartbroken, paralyzed by the loss of his beloved. He asked how to be relieved from such longing. I replied by reminding him that longing lies at the heart of our human experience, and added:

> Remember, in the wisdom of your culture, *Pothos* (longing) is always present, along with *Eros* (love) and *Himeros* (desire). All testify to our incompleteness. That is not the problem. The problem is when we transfer these inner drives onto the Other.

No wonder we suffer with their loss.

Suffering is inescapable. The question, though, invariably comes back to me: *what does that make me do, or keep me from doing?*

That is where my/your responsibility begins. You have to move forward with your new agendas, not merely transfer them to a new beloved person, but go further into your life with unfulfilled desire. If ever you feel wholly fulfilled, you have either become a god, or have died.

The central challenge of my book *The Eden Project*—that title metaphorically recalls our longing for the original union, the primal unity—is: *what am I asking of the other that I need to ask of myself?* The first paragraph of that book reminds us that the third member of the couple standing at the altar is Death, for sooner or later one of them will suffer loss. It is not a cheery thought, but it happens to be accurate, and makes the relationship all the more precious while still present.

EMC: On the back of my 1967 edition of *The Poems of Doctor Zhivago*, there is a black-and-white photograph of Boris Pasternak in a dark suit, his inscrutable head framed against a window, like a prisoner, through which fragments of an indistinct outside world are visible. Below the image, a fragment of his poem *March* appears:

> O nights, O passing days and nights!
> The drip from eaves and window sills,
> The thinning icicles on gables,
> The chatter of unsleeping rills!

Whenever I look at that back cover, I sense his solitude, and also his loneliness. Pasternak saw solitude as both necessary and costly, a state that brought clarity but also carried the risk of estrangement. Solitude gave him the space to think, to work outside the demands of power, to hold onto his own way of seeing. For him, creativity required solitude—a space apart from distraction, where thought could deepen and art could take shape.

When he was awarded the Nobel Prize in 1958 for *Doctor Zhivago*, the Soviet government saw it as an act of defiance, as the novel had been banned in the country. At first, he accepted the honor. Then came the denunciations, threats of exile, and former colleagues turning against him. The Soviet Writers' Union condemned Pasternak, and the state made it clear that his family's safety was at risk. Under these conditions, he was forced to decline the prize, and the ordeal left him isolated, reinforcing the themes of exile and integrity that had shaped his work. This isolation was not unfamiliar to him. His letters with Marina Tsvetaeva had already revealed how solitude, rather than being a retreat, could become a condition of thought, a space where language stretched toward what was otherwise unreachable. In *The Same Solitude: Boris Pasternak and Marina Tsvetaeva*, Catherine Ciepiela traces the correspondence between two poets bound by distance, exile, and the pressures of history. Their solitude was not just absence but a medium through which their ideas on poetry, history, and the self were tested and refined. The letters do not ease their isolation so much as clarify it, sharpening their sense of what poetry could hold, and what it could salvage.

Solitude is not loneliness, though (as I will consider shortly) many of us struggle to distinguish them. Solitude usually involves choice, a refuge where thought and spirit are free to unfold. Loneliness, on the other hand, is what remains when choice is taken away, when there is a lack of connection with others or with ourselves. Pasternak had to live with both. In his final years, he was watched, vilified, abandoned by those who had once called him a friend. He lived to see the deaths of Marina Tsvetaeva, Osip Mandelstam, and Vladimir Mayakovsky, all part of his literary world. Each of their deaths was marked by tragedy, and Pasternak, who had managed to survive Stalin's purges and repression, was deeply affected by their fates. The solitude that had once been a sanctuary became the confinement of someone no longer permitted to belong.

For the most part, during my childhood, I was at ease with solitude. But as I observed the people around me and encountered the thinkers, writers, and artists I came to admire, I recognized in many of them—Pasternak among them—a possessive loneliness that would not leave them, even in the company of loved ones. Sometimes it had been with them from the start, and, other times, it festered within them like a slow-growing illness. In adolescence, my fear of the connection between solitude and loneliness—which in Spanish are the same word, *soledad*—merged with the questions of self and belonging, convincing me that loneliness was an inherent aspect of the human condition and that solitude, rather than companionship or distraction, was the only authentic way to live with it. Over time, life experiences, along with the support of my work, my mentors, and the timely guidance of Buddhist writings in my early twenties, helped me separate the value of solitude from the affliction of loneliness. For me, and, I suspect, for many of us, that separation remains, and perhaps will always remain, an ongoing concern.

Since those days, solitude has been an invaluable ally in my life and my intellectual and artistic practices. It has prevented distractions and created the space for deep attention not only to the work itself but to what remains unresolved around it. Solitude has helped me be present, not by adding anything, but by removing distractions from my attention. The big transitions in my practice have been served by time spent in solitude. These shifts don't always start in solitude. Sometimes the spark that has ignited them was kindled in the middle of a crowd or a frenetic moment in my life. Regardless of how they begin, it is in solitude that I sort out what's being asked of me, my life, and my work.

Although solitude often requires physical isolation, ultimately, it is about a way of being. What matters is not so much where one is but how one is there. Solitude is not detachment but a way to facilitate presence. In our interconnected and busy lives, however, solitude is hard to find, especially the kind that remains undisturbed by news, opinions, and demands. Many of us struggle to pay attention to the quieter spaces within ourselves, where strength and clarity emerge. I can't think of a time more hostile to solitude than ours, and I worry that the conditions for it will only worsen.

Today, retreating into the woods or walking along a deserted beach, seeking a space to dwell with ourselves, is complicated by the fact that anyone can reach us at any time. The phones most of us carry are always accessible, whether to others or to our own curiosity, our need to check emails, videos, texts, or news. For many, this attachment and desire to stay connected is so strong that solitude becomes a burden. The fear of missing out, and the nagging thought of who might be trying to reach us or what might be happening elsewhere intrude on solitude. Rather than settling into it, we count the minutes until we can return to the world and our connections. When solitude is seen as an imposition, a struggle marked by thoughts of what we could be doing or who we could be talking to, it is neither empowering nor rewarding. The encroachment of social networks and devices on what little solitude we are able to find reflects a broader shift in society, a growing reluctance to engage in an open, unbounded relationship with solitude itself.

As an artist, I recognize that these noises of our era, amplified by the expectations of people and markets inherent in my career, create an environment that only a deliberate and conscientious practice that recognizes the necessity of solitude can endure. Creativity is not simply—or mostly—an act of making but of deepening, of searching, of recognizing and moving toward something not fully formed. That movement requires a space where distractions are minimized, where the pressures of expectation, convention, or external validation are quieted.

Creativity depends on attentiveness, both to what is happening within us and to our interaction with whatever we are working on. Even in the roughest, most aggressive creative work, nuance and subtle recognition are essential. If, despite being alone, our minds are cluttered with thoughts of what we should be doing, what is popular or respected, what worked yesterday, what we might want to do tomorrow, or with finances and other external concerns, then solitude is too fraught to allow for the introspection and discovery that creative work requires. For me, what I seek in solitude is the reduction of inputs that distract me and pull me away from the present. Without solitude, the possibilities of the work and the richness, clarity, and discoveries it might bring remain obscured by the disquiet within myself.

Ralph Waldo Emerson saw solitude in a similar way, not as withdrawal but as a space where the mind can free itself from external influence and encounter its own depths. He writes in his essay *Self Reliance*: "It is easy in the world to live after the world's opinion; it is easy in solitude to live after our own; but the great man is he who in the midst of the crowd keeps with perfect sweetness the independence of solitude."

Yet not all solitude is the same. If Emerson's solitude allows for self-examination, for refining thought and intention before re-engaging with the world, there is another kind that forces a confrontation with what is beyond individual will. A poet I admire, Robinson Jeffers, understood this. For him, solitude was not a way of strengthening the self but of dissolving it, of moving beyond human preoccupations into the larger forces of nature. For Jeffers, solitude was not isolation but a shedding of sentimentality and self-importance. He did not seek solitude to cultivate an interior world, as Emerson did, but to step outside of human illusions altogether. In "The Answer," he writes:

> Organic wholeness, the wholeness of life and things, the divine beauty of the universe. Love that, not man
> Apart from that, or else you will share man's pitiful confusions, or drown in despair when his days darken.

This solitude is not a retreat from but a confrontation with reality. Jeffers built Tor House, a stone house on a bluff overlooking the Pacific in Carmel, California, with his own hands, where I have had the privilege of spending some time. For him, it was a family home where he could write, be with nature, and share his life with his wife, Una, and their twins. The solitude he sought was not an escape from society but a way to step back from its distractions and attune himself to the enduring and elemental forces of the natural world. Where Emerson saw solitude as a means of refining the inner life, Jeffers saw it as a stripping away of the self, a recognition that we are part of something greater than ourselves.

While they seem different, there's not really a contradiction between the value that Jeffers and Emerson found in solitude, and both perspectives have shaped my own. There are times when solitude sharpens my vision, when the silence of the studio allows me to see more clearly what is in front of me. Other times, solitude unsettles me, forces me to sit with doubt, with uncertainty about the work, its direction, and its necessity. Both are valuable. Clarity is not always immediate, nor is it always comfortable. But I have found that the uncertainty that arises in solitude has a role. It checks my hubris and challenges whatever territories I assumed I have secured. In my experience, the solitude that leads to awareness, deep calmness, and clarity is not a state to be achieved, or some sort of retreat, but a process of carrying nothing extra so that the conversation between ourselves and the world can be attended to.

The second question asked whether there have been moments when solitude has clarified or intensified my vision. I can recall instances of purposeful extended solitude, such as my time at the lighthouse when I was deciding to become an artist, or the time I spent at Dartmouth College after my divorce, where apart from visits twice a month to see my children, I spent most of those nine months working and immersed in nature, alone. But while those examples are perhaps notable, solitude for me is a daily practice, and the quality of my life and work depend on it. Being an artist is largely a solitary endeavor with limited interaction with others. I am grateful for this solitude and the attention it allows, giving me the time and space to focus on work that is, for the most part, meaningful and will eventually be shared. What I hope for in my practice is not to create from solitude, but through it. Solitude is a way of making space for presence, for whatever wants to drop in, for what remains unresolved, for what asks to be seen. It sharpens and unsettles, intensifies and softens, altering what we see and what we feel.

Not everyone has, or has had, the choice of solitude, and I recognize my fortune in both having this choice and being able to accept it. Many have had their lives invaded, their private world stripped of the dignity of being alone in peace. Some, struggling with fear, pain, catastrophe, or war, cannot choose solitude. Others, like Pasternak, struggled to hold on to themselves as the world tried to take them away. In "Hamlet," from *The Poems of Doctor Zhivago*, he asks to be left alone, to not be swept into the theater of history:

> I am fond of this Thy stubborn project,
> And to play my part I am content.
> But another drama is in progress,
> And, this once, O let me be exempt.

His plea, "O let me be exempt," is both a reminder of what we so often take for granted and a recognition of the gift that it is to be able to commune with solitude.

9

What is attention, and how do you decide where to direct it? Have there been periods in your life or career when you paid attention to aspects of the world different from those you focus on today?

Attention is the rarest and purest form of generosity.

Simone Weil

EMC: Attention is how we direct consciousness, shaping what enters our awareness. This direction establishes our engagement with the world, allowing perception to sharpen and meaning to emerge. Attention can be narrow, and in our preference for quick results, it often is, but even when we focus on a limited aim, the rest of the world, our senses, and our history do not entirely fade into the background. They remain as context and operators influencing perception in ways we may not immediately recognize, shaping the depth and texture of what we think we are seeing, hearing, and understanding. Perception is formed by attention, by the openness or resistance with which we meet the world. To attend is to participate, to allow what is before us to reveal itself rather than imposing our expectations upon it. Yet much of what shapes us happens beyond our directed awareness. Accidents, encounters, and unnoticed details alter our course in ways we may only recognize later.

The relationship between attention, perception, deliberateness, and accidents has been explored by many people more capable than me. For example, here is a beautiful, indirect reference to them by Okakura Kakuzō's *The Book of Tea*:

> Flower stories are endless. We shall recount but one more. In the sixteenth century the morning-glory was as yet a rare plant with us. Rikiu had an entire garden planted with it, which he cultivated with assiduous care. The fame of his convolvuli reached the ear of the Taiko, and he expressed a desire to see them, in consequence of which Rikiu invited him to a morning tea at his house. On the appointed day Taiko walked through the garden, but nowhere could he see any vestige of the convolvulus. The ground had been leveled and strewn with fine pebbles and sand. With sullen anger the despot entered the tea-room, but a sight waited him there which completely restored his humour. On the tokonoma, in a rare bronze of Sung workmanship, lay a single morning-glory—the queen of the whole garden!

Attention could dwell on that single bloom. It is the garden, and the garden is it. Rather than being about focusing, about narrowing attention, this passage attends to nuances, not only the flower itself but also its fleetingness, presence, beauty, connections, historical context, and role in the tea ceremony. Taiko's disappointment and anger dissolved at the sight of the morning glory. What we attend to, we make real. What we neglect fades. To attend is to recognize significance. Attention shapes the structure of experience.

But where to direct it? In the story, the answer seems clear, but the choice is not always easy or conscious. Since attention is constantly directed by habit, urgency, desire, and fear, we tend to mistake what demands attention for what deserves it. Many things in our world claim our attention, and so it can be squandered or cultivated. A hurried glance is not the same as a sustained gaze. An instrumental focus is not the same as an open presence. If attention is the means by which we meet the world, then the way we attend determines the depth and richness of that encounter. Attention shifts over time. The things that once seemed urgent recede. What seemed secondary becomes central.

I have always been interested in many things—physics, art, literature, philosophy, architecture, teaching, family—but I don't get distracted easily, which has allowed me to sustain these multiple interests while dedicating focused time to each. But my attention is different now than it used to be.

When I was younger, I worried about these multiple interests, which I saw as competing with one another for my time. There was little sense within me that these were part of a whole. Instead, I treated them, and all my other concerns and observations, mostly as independent from one another. It was as if I looked at the world through different windows without realizing these windows were all part of the same house. Even so, though often siloed and lacking important context, my attention allowed me to accumulate some knowledge and a measure of self-awareness.

One of the greatest gifts of maturing has been the growing understanding that everything I do and am interested in is part of an ecosystem of attention that, in turn, reflects who I am. This understanding has revealed connections between teaching and writing, physics and spirit, art and speaking to my children, building a house and poetry, connections I would not have anticipated when I once saw my varied interests as competing. Looking at my career, I see two surprising things: all my major early interests are still present in what I do today, and one of the most distinctive aspects of my work is precisely this multi-faceted approach to creativity and meaning.

Along with this integration came a different kind of attention. My earlier, narrowly focused attention evolved into a broader consideration. In all areas of my life, I began to value the interconnections between events and to allow for what I knew I didn't know, as well as for what I didn't know I didn't know. Instead of processing everything through the strongest single lens I could find, I increasingly relied on an assembly of lenses, each accounting for a different aspect of reality and of myself. In some way, this is like having no lenses at all.

This shift in attention is not just a matter of broadening one's view but of reorienting perception itself. There is a way of attending that isolates, categorizes, and reduces, seeking certainty and control, and this way is useful and necessary in many aspects of life. There is another way of attending that is receptive rather than seizing, that does not seek to fix what it perceives but instead allows it to unfold. This way of attending does not merely analyze relationships but experiences them as a living whole, where meaning arises not from discrete parts but from their interplay. Instead of things, everything becomes a process. The most profound transformations in thought, in art, and in life happen when this second mode of attention is cultivated, allowing for a reality that is richer, more integrated, and more attuned to the world as it actually is.

To be an artist is first to ask what art is and then to bring an answer about, both of which are difficult. Clarity in one helps the other. Confusion in one hinders the other. Most of what we see that looks like art is not art, and more often than not, this is because attention was not paid to the question or its answer. But what kind of attention is needed here? It would not be the attention that merely dissects a problem into parts, looking for a formulaic solution, nor the kind that imposes predetermined structures onto the work. Instead, it would be an attention that is open, relational, and responsive, one that allows the work to emerge in a way that could not have been fully anticipated.

What I mean by attention to the question *what is art?* is not a narrow or explicit test we must pass before working. Rather, it is an attention that considers the question before, during, and after a work of art is brought into being. It is an attention that accounts for subtle emotional and intellectual nuances. It senses inauthenticity and when something does not feel right. It can observe without attachment and also measure devotion, without which art rarely happens. This kind of attention does not demand immediate resolution. It lingers in ambiguity, in complexity, in the space where contradictions coexist. It allows art to be more than an act of making, it becomes an act of perceiving, of encountering the world as it is rather than as we expect it to be.

The struggle between these modes of attention is not limited to art. It is present in how we approach life. The impulse to categorize and control, to make rigid distinctions and impose certainty, is always at odds with the need to remain open, to allow for uncertainty and emergence. But only in the latter space, where things are held in dynamic relation rather than forced into resolution, does meaning arise in a way that is alive. The task, then, is not simply to seek answers but to cultivate a way of attending that keeps the world, and ourselves, from becoming fixed, lifeless, and closed off to what might still be discovered.

JH: Where we direct our attention, where we spend our energy, varies of course according to the stage of life and the context in which we find ourselves. There was a time when learning to control our arms and legs, rise to our feet, and wobbly walk occupied our attention. In the current adult life, our attention is typically contending on a daily basis both in responding to incoming messages and accountabilities and by establishing priorities for ourselves.

In an ideal world, we could direct energies and priorities in an equally balanced pie chart with quadrants. Quadrant 1 would be the focus we direct to the people in our lives, especially partner and family. Quadrant 2 would be the world of work whether it be homemaking or a day job. Part of being a functional adult is the capacity and accountability in supporting oneself and those to whom one is committed. The younger one is, the more this sector demands our energy. My early work life was devoted to college teaching, and occasional administration in the humanities. In the years after retraining as a Jungian analyst I carried forty plus therapy clients per week plus public speaking on week days or frequent weekends. Presently that load is cut back to fewer than twenty cases and several Zoom presentations per month. Quadrant 3 is one's relationship to the world around: friends, socializing, volunteer work, and various citizenship obligations. This includes staying *au courant*. I read several newspapers a day in hand or online for I think it a duty for a citizen in a democracy to remain informed. (As the motto of *The Washington Post* has it, "Democracy Dies in Darkness.") Additionally, I receive a large amount of email traffic from interested folks who have read a book, heard a podcast, seen a YouTube program, or have a question. I try to respond to all. Quadrant 4 is that section devoted to the cultivation of a dialogue with the soul, and, if it does not sound grandiose, with the cosmos as well. This includes for me working with my dreams, occasional active imagination sessions, reading, and writing.

Writing for me is an essential part of personal growth. I do not know what I think, feel, and believe about something until I try to articulate it to others. Then a lot of sorting and sifting occurs. Sometimes the ego is in charge of that process, making editorial and stylistic changes, and sometimes the numinous is in charge. While none of us, and in no single day, may find the perfect balance of quadrants I have suggested here, it remains a goal. I do find more and more that my introverted soul wishes more time and energy for that fourth quadrant, perhaps as a consequence of living in Hotel Terminus and recognizing that my life trajectory is currently on the glide path downward toward some kind of landing at Mortality Field.

It is consonant with my current stage of life that the claims of the outer world fade in urgency, and the questions of what this journey is about, what needs still to be addressed, and how we might revision what this life has been about grow more and more pressing. The majority of clients in my current practice are over sixty years old, not by my design, but because we have generally been together for some while. Of my current case load, I would say only three are being directed by a needful response to some psychopathology, namely, a set of symptoms that require immediate attendance. Jung said that as he grew older he was less and less interested in psychopathology and more and more in the approach to the numinous. It is true that matters of physical health are frequent topics of focus. I had one patient die in the last two weeks, two be diagnosed with cancer, and two have other significant health issues emerge. It is also consonant with the stage of life that four are dealing with the loss of their partners and the huge gulf that opens in their lives.

But what I also find interesting is that their dreams seldom speak to these present matters. Rather, they most often bring up experiences from the past. At first one might be tempted to think of this phenomenon as some form of nostalgia, or perhaps still a processing of life's traumata, or review of roads not taken. And some are that. But I have also concluded in these dreams that the psyche continues to rework the "story" of one's life. Having written on the assemblage of our "false," self, that is the adaptive self, elsewhere, and having written elsewhere about trauma, let me just summarize here the importance of "story" in our "sense of self."

I say "sense of self" because that limited purview is all we have available to consciousness. In any given moment we are in the grip of a complex of some sort, even as we also may be influenced by someone else's projection upon us. The Self, capital *S*, as Jungians understand it, is an organic phenomenon, an energy system transcendent to consciousness, though it includes consciousness as an epiphenomenon. One of the characteristics of this Self is a deep determination to make sense of the raw data of our experiences. From infancy on we ask: what was that, who are you, what is the transaction occurring here, and what is its message to me? Our story making is sometimes conscious, other times not. We learn not to touch a hot pan, to look both ways before crossing a street, and other stories that are protective. But even more we evolve stories that curb our natural, healthy drives and divide us against ourselves. Part of what psychoanalysis is about is the discernment of such "stories" that are running our lives, bringing them into more conscious awareness, and seeking to write a larger story than those generated by our history. As I have told many a patient, we would not turn our automobile over an eight-year-old, but the story evolved by the eight-year-old we were is one of those driving our contemporary lives.

When we examine the dream motifs in my age bracket, I find the women's dreams are mostly about other people, namely relationships. (All of my current female clients are still involved in the helping professions.) And men's dreams mostly involve their former work contexts. Obviously there are other people there, but they seem less germane than the various pressures, trials, and expectations that work environments exacted of them. But in both genders, the "stories" seem to me to be the real subject matter. So, an unofficial protocol has emerged involving these questions. 1) How did you understand what happened back then? 2) How did it get "storied" in your life thereafter? 3) What did that "story" make you do, or what did it keep you from doing? And lastly, how do you understand the event, situation, or "story" today, given your larger range of experiences and greater knowledge of yourself now?

Needless to say, I ask the same questions of myself, whether as I see a parallel in the life of a client, or I have my own dream, or when I examine my patterns with their implicit stories. And it is most likely that I am then in that liminal zone between Quadrants 2 and 4, the spheres of work and exploration of soul.

When I use the word *soul*, I intend it both as the literal translation of the Greek word *psyche* and the inexplicable mystery we all embody. As we consider more carefully what our values are, why we hold them instead of others, and where our limited energies should be distributed, we are performing a psychotherapeutic praxis.

The etymology of psychotherapy means "to attend, care for the soul." All of the four Quadrants may be arenas tended psychotherapeutically, or none of them. A huge amount of the tenor of modern first and second world culture is about distraction, numbing, and the search for new sensations, all of which are counter to psychotherapy, for they separate one from oneself, and the urgent question of what is one called to at that stage of their journey. Such citizens of Contemporea live "the distracted life." So what is it about this summons to accountability for this brief space between the mysteries that requires distraction? And if the "treatment plan" for what ails us, or intimidates us, or which asks that we work harder at something takes us away from the work of soul, then is it possible that we did not show up for our lives?

What I can say with complete conviction is that the quality of our lives will never be more evolved than our relationship with our inner life. If one is looking to the world out there to learn who we are, then one is likely to succumb to the noisiest, most troubled among us. As Jung wrote of Hitler, in a disordered time, the people chose the most disordered among them to be their leader, and he led them across the rooftops like a Pied Piper till they fell into the streets below and broke their backs. The most inadequate, the most empty, the most disturbed among us will rise to be our leader when enough of us have abrogated our summons to consciousness and accountability. That is why attention to that fourth Quadrant, the dialogue with the soul, and one's place and purpose in this cosmos, is so critical, not only to our well-being but to democracy as well.

10

How do you decide when it is right to continue to deepen your exploration of a territory and when it is time to let go and explore something else?

Traveler, there is no path,
the path is made by walking.

Antonio Machado

JH: One of the measures of moral adulthood seems to me to be the ability to dig in and carry through on responsibilities whether one wishes to or not. The stunning changes, in first world nations at least, of lifestyles, and the many comforts, conveniences, and distractions available creates in all of us the slow percolation of an attitude that life ought to flow smoothly and pleasantly, and irritation when it does not. Our material abundance is very seductive. Yet it was not long ago that the life of most people was, in the words of the English writer Thomas Hobbes, "solitary, poor, nasty, brutish, and short." My own parents labored weekdays and weekends to bring food to the table, and their parents worked in fields or died in coal mines.

One of the finest educational tools for anyone is surely having to do a job that one hates, and yet has to do it. It helps one develop discipline to show up because one has to, and it may increase one's compassion for those who have no choice. I hated working in a factory, wearing steel-toed shoes, safety glasses, in 100+ degree heat, flush with flying shards of metal. But my father worked there all his adult life, and never complained. He had migraine headaches but never complained. For him the work was not a choice; it was an iron-bound necessity. Once when walking out of the factory as August neared its brutal end, I thoughtlessly said, "I will be glad when August is over so I can go back to college." He replied quietly, "For me, August never ends." That was a report from him, not a complaint. Having seen the alternative, I knew that my ticket out, education, was my good luck, not my merit. So, later in life, while retraining in Switzerland, I taught English and cleaned houses without complaint because I knew I was lucky. There has never been a day in my adult life that I ever took my privilege for granted. I still don't.

Earlier in graduate school, I drove into downtown Newark, NJ for German lessons to pass required exams before I could go the next step in school. During the summers, I drove my wife to her graduate school north of Newark, then down to New Brunswick to Rutgers to take additional graduate classes, back to Newark teach a class for the NJ Commission for the Blind preparing handicapped students for college, then back up to fetch my spouse, and then back to my graduate campus to prepare for graduate classes and teaching the next day. It was approximately 150 miles in North Jersey's massive traffic, and all in one day, every day. But I never complained because I remembered I wasn't in a factory, and I was doing this for my future.

Separately, I was testing, and being tested, on whether a life of scholarship was right for me. I loved teaching, and had no choice but to demonstrate a capacity for research if I were to get a degree to teach at the university level, but I did not love scholarship. For one thing, a life of scholarship, because of the burden of discovery which builds on the work of others, was tedious, even boring. It required that I study more and more about less and less, and cut off the collateral interests that proved most attractive. This was what had earlier accounted for my high school and early college academic mediocrity. When later a professor, I tried several times to start scholarly studies and abandoned ship within months. I did not write for twenty years. Something within was refusing to move forward. I do not think this was a standard writer's block. Rather, it was something in me that was resisting the "publish or perish" mandate.

One of the principles of psychoanalysis is to respect resistance, though not to collude with it. Usually resistance is in direct proportion to the anxieties one stirs up in moving forward. Thus, smoking those anxieties out, teasing them into fears instead, is part of the analytic work. Anxieties obscure the road ahead; fears are the specific roadblocks that one is then called upon to address. In my case, I do not think the resistance was anxiety, really. The fear was real, though: boredom and wasting one's precious life energy on something in which my soul was not invested. As I look back on those years up to the present, it all looks as if it was planned. It wasn't. But

I can see the invisible hand that played a role, an inner determination to only spend my intellectual curiosity and commitment of energy to something that really mattered to me. After retraining in analytic psychology, twenty plus books emerged.

These days, with their number diminishing rapidly, I am even more committed to this principle of conservation of energy. Within civilized limits, I only spend energy on something which delights, moves, frightens, or tantalizes the soul. I don't have to ask what that is, because that determination is usually available to me in a very short time. But that makes it all sound as if I am in charge. Frankly, I think it is the little people again. They put up road blocks at their discretion and open the gates when they wish to. I just happen to have learned to follow their directions, most of the time.

Generically speaking, my account here probably feels too familiar to the reader. We all have to do things we do not wish to do. And we all have things we believe we want to do. I cannot tell how many folks have said to me, "I always wanted to write a novel," or "I always wanted to learn Italian," or "I plan to learn to play the piano," but it never happens. Most of the time our good intentions are scattered along the highway. Why is that the case? The excuses are plentiful: "The kids take too much time," "I am too tired at the end of the day," "I am afraid I have no talent," and so on. All of these excuses might be true. But if we look at them, they remain excuses. If we are conscious on the proverbial death bed, it is far less likely that we will perseverate on the wrong things we did than those we wished but did not do. I have often made that point to folks expressing frustration over the unlived life, and sometimes it even works for them and gets them off the dime.

But through the years, an even bigger perspective has become insistent for me. Speaking very generally, the first half of our lives is spent trying to serve what the world asks, expects, of us: namely, to be social beings, self-sufficient, and productive in whatever arena. But I think the second half is more about what wants to enter the world through us. This is not just in the sectors of creative endeavor but in terms of our personality development. We are all the carriers of the life force endowed by nature. Is it not a terrible thing when we do not find the courage or commitment to serve it, or when we are blocked by social conditions as so often has happened to humans through the centuries? Something within the soul of such unfortunates withers and dies then, even as the body may carry on for many more years.

There are many key indicators we have from nature that communicate to us the desires of the soul, desires that may have little to do with the ego's plans. One of course is the feeling function. We can do all "the right things" in the first half of life and find it empty, as so often is the case. When we are tracking a course right for whatever is seeking expression through us, we may encounter all sorts of outer difficulties, but the feeling flow, the inherent rightness of things is there supporting us. Similarly, energy systems serve or oppose us. We can will our energies in the many directions, and life often requires that we do so, but if we continue such spiritual violence it always leads to depression, self-medication, or anger referred to others. Most of all, meaning is found when we serve the soul, even if there is a price to pay for such service. Most of the people we admire in history did not have easy lives, or the acceptance of their coevals, but we admire them because they served some values that wished expression through them.

Imagine this situation: your time on this planet is limited—only 4,000 weeks as my friend Oliver Burkeman has calculated—and you do have choices, if you are willing to fight for them, and something larger than your comfort or even understanding wants expression through you. Why you, you might ask? Why not? That is not our choice. Our choice is whether we pay attention (*therapeuein*: to listen or attend + *psyche*: the soul). Our choice is whether we can open to a larger definition of our journey than may be comfortable to those around us, or to ourselves. I have often said to clients "of every choice, every juncture in your life, ask yourself this question: does this path make me larger, or does it diminish me?" Usually you already know the answer to that question. If you do not, keep asking. Having then discerned the real issue, choose the path of enlargement. This is not about enlarging the ego. Quite the contrary, this is often humbling to the ego. And risky. What it does mean is that when one has taken such risks as the soul asks of us, you will find something with supporting you even if the rest of the world does not. You will find you are living a larger story, and that is humbling, but in the end it makes all the struggle worthwhile.

EMC: We often hear that success comes from relentless focus, that greatness is earned by those who stay with one pursuit and do not let go. The idea that discipline and constancy alone lead to mastery is an appealing notion because it suggests a plan that we can follow. But a life narrowed to a single aim can also become rigid, blind to what lies beyond its tunnel of purpose. The question, then, is not simply how to persist, but how to discern when persistence turns into confinement. How do we know when to deepen our exploration of a territory and when to let it go, to allow movement, renewal, and change?

The process of discovery and creativity in my work as an artist often begins with one idea, then shifts to another, sometimes quite different from the first. These iterations might continue for weeks, months, and occasionally years, an evolution that was also true of my scientific work, a process that requires the discipline of perseverance and the art of letting go.

The dynamics between perseverance and letting go encompass various attributes, factors, and qualities that are obvious to anyone who has tried to accomplish something meaningful, while others are subtle, nuanced, and difficult to pin down. The discipline of perseverance, for instance, seems most effective when we can be fully invested in the work, resilient to the challenges that arise—including fatigue and failure—without losing the ability to remain detached enough to question our investment and look for something better if it's available to us. Knowing when to continue, when to stop, or when to step away often depends on our capacity for attachment and detachment, our sense of purpose, and our awareness of what we pay attention to and why.

Neither the discipline of perseverance nor the art of letting go came naturally to me. Like many children, I would start something, then move on to the next thing. That restlessness, in addition to being part of the playfulness and roving attention of childhood, wasn't unusual. even for adults, in the society I grew up in.

The Cuba of my childhood was caught between the reinvention of the revolution and disillusionment with what it had once promised. In everyday life, that tension meant food shortages, few toys, little knowledge of the world beyond our island, and billboards and television urging us to "do the right thing" for the revolution. Most of the people I knew seemed publicly anxious and privately disillusioned, but always restless. In my family, these feelings were amplified and twisted into sadness by the looming prospect of exile, so restlessness and dreaminess became two of the few outlets left for a kid.

My focus only settled on a few pursuits: playing with toy soldiers that once belonged to my uncle, drawing, and planning pranks, usually on my brother. But the combined forces of exile, the strict methods of traditional Cuban child-rearing, the demands of Catholic priests, and my parents' insistence on academic excellence, whether or not it suited my natural inclinations, hammered discipline into me.

Perseverance is an elusive concept for a child. How much effort is enough? How much more should I push?

How long should I study, practice a sport, or work on this drawing? Have I done enough?

During most of my childhood, I never found my own answers to these questions, but adults had one consistent answer for me: the bar was always higher than where I was. More was always expected. Now, half a century later, I can't tell if I really had any natural tendency for perseverance or if it was almost entirely imposed from the outside. Whatever the source, perseverance did become part of my personality, so that by my teenage years, I was disciplined, resilient, and prepared to persevere, even if at the cost of other aspects of my life.

Whether perseverance came naturally to me or not, it was certainly encouraged and admired. Letting go, on the other hand, wasn't even part of the conversation. It meant being a coward, a quitter, or betraying yourself and your family. Yet when I think about our situation, it's strange that no one praised, let alone talked about, the idea of letting go. We were exiles, after all. We had given up an entire life and family with the idea that leaving our country would improve our lives. There was also something central about letting go in Catholicism. The Church constantly reminded us of the need to release things we held dear, often calling them sinful.

Perhaps the reason letting go was never mentioned is that I was born in a country trying to reinvent itself, where everyone had to be committed to the dream that was the revolution, and in this commitment there was no room for ambivalence. Then we were exiled to a place where, if you didn't persevere, you'd sink into despair and poverty. In both contexts, letting go seemed a concession to the forces of evil. So even in my undisciplined moments as a child, I might not have known how to persevere, but I never thought letting go was an option. And if other people did, it was mostly in their hearts, not in anything I could see. At least not then.

My parents held on to their marriage despite all odds. They persevered for us, their children, for Catholic values, for social expectations. The lesson I received was, *you've made your bed, now lie in it.* Growing up as a boy in the Caribbean and later as a foreigner in Spain, frequently having to fight with other kids to prove I wouldn't quit or show fear, I came to see that fearlessness and never letting go were linked. In my mind, as in the minds of many around me, letting go meant giving in to fear; it was a sign you didn't have the strength or toughness to keep going. It didn't occur to me then that fear was often fueling perseverance—the fear of the unknown, of failing to meet expectations, fears that kept me holding on and blind to most things outside the path I was supposed to follow. Mine was certainly not a context that allowed for learning how to let go, but there are few environments that teach letting go in an empowering way.

This empowered letting go is not easy to teach because it requires judgments that are intuitive, uncharted, and grounded in self-knowledge. Letting go calls for sensitivity to timing, awareness of limits, and an openness to possibilities beyond effort or control. It's more about perception than prescription, demanding a certain fluidity, a readiness to release without regret, to see an end not as defeat but as completion. Unlike the discipline of perseverance, it is difficult to know when the capacity for letting go has waned, or even what letting go truly means in a given situation. Sometimes, the very act of letting go, virtuous in one instance, can appear as monstrous abandonment in another.

Painting is a good teacher on both perseverance and letting go. I start paintings with very little to go on. Sometimes I have nothing but a vague feeling. Other times, it is a mysterious resonance between two elements. I prefer to start my work driven by impulses or insights I don't understand. It is never a process of communicating or teaching something I know or believe. Instead, it an exploration hoping for a discovery that is never guaranteed. It is a lot like going for a walk in a forest one doesn't know. This is a forest walk not to find something significant hiding between trees or something about myself, but to bring about, or bring closer, the truth of the totality that is the forest, the world, and me. There are no maps for this, so getting lost is inevitably part of the process, as it is a different type of guidance than the one that takes us somewhere when we have a map or previous knowledge of where we are going.

Perseverance is critical in sustaining effort and enduring failure and fatigue in this exploration, and also in accepting being lost without running back or shooting flares into the air for something or someone to rescue us. I am willing to work and rework a painting as long as there's a sense that my engagement is still meaningful, that something worthwhile is both in the present and around the corner. Guided more by feeling and intuition than by what I know about art or life, I continue to deepen this exploration, which sometimes requires destroying what I have done. In these destructions and corrections, knowing how to let go means accepting the losses without allowing them to exhaust me.

Perseverance works alongside our ability to let go by keeping us engaged and committed, not to the time or successes we've invested, nor to the goals we might have formulated, but to what is possible, in the promise suggested by the act of exploration. I have many reminders around me to keep me from convincing myself that something facile or non-transforming is the truth I am after. It is easy to come up with lies, so the discipline of perseverance is not only about not giving up, but also about remaining vigilant against our deceptions and disillusionment.

When something shows me that there's no longer truth in my exploration nor around the corner, then I know it is time to let go entirely. This radical letting go sometimes feels like a death and sometimes like a rebirth, but it is always the ending of something and the beginning of something else that has yet to unfold. This is true in painting and it is true in life. Many careers and many marriages end, or ought to end, when we realize we are at the end of the road of meaning, when truth for us is no longer in that path. We might not know what will happen next or if we will find a better path, but we know we have to let go.

Spirit, Meaning, Purpose, and The Unknown

11

What characterizes the life of the spirit as you see and define it? And what then is soul?

> If you are losing your soul and you know it,
> then you still have a soul to lose.
>
> Charles Bukowski

EMC: On a cold fall afternoon eight years ago, I went for a walk along a forested bank of the Connecticut River, as I often did when I was working at Dartmouth College. It was not a vast, untamed wilderness, but the concentration of white pines and hemlocks and the sounds of birds and creaking trees gave the feeling of a much thicker forest. The trail went over a bridge, by a muddy path where beetles, mushrooms, and rain were helping old fallen trees rot, and down a hill where the ground began to brown with pine needles, letting me know I was nearing my favorite part of the hike.

As I came around the turn marked by two boulders, the forest opened, offering a view of pale blue and gold water framed by bare branches, with the low sun casting long beams that made the surface of the river shimmer. I'm sure there were noises other than the rush of the river, but I couldn't hear any until a sudden gust of wind swept through, lifting dead leaves from the ground and sending them into the air with a dry, rustling sound. This momentary unraveling of the stillness felt as though it was sensing the spirit of the forest and that it was sensing me. When the wind passed, silence settled again, and the shadows stretching across the water seemed longer. The night was coming.

As I stood there not yet wanting to leave, the moment became deeper, vaster, and the separation between me and everything else faded. The place and I were one.

We remained inseparable until the call of a blue jay brought me back to myself. That oneness was probably what I would call soul, and maybe this story is as good an explanation as I can offer about spirit and soul, but let me try to say more.

The spirit and the soul are not separate entities but different aspects of the same reality. The spirit is the energy that animates life, the movement that we see in the changing forms of the world and feel in the pull of our own lives toward connection and meaning. It is not distant or abstract but present, unfolding in the patterns and rhythms of being. The soul is the stillness within movement, the awareness that observes without clinging or resisting. Together, the spirit and the soul reveal different ways of being. The spirit reaches outward, engaging with the world, while the soul remains inward, grounding us in reflection and presence.

The life of the spirit is not separate from the tangible world but exists as a deeper level of Being. It draws us beyond the immediate and measurable, defined by a sense of connection—both to ourselves and to something larger. The spirit thrives in the recognition that in losing ourselves, we find ourselves, and that in giving, we receive. It moves us toward wholeness and meaning, inviting an intuitive awareness of the whole while resisting the tendency to dissect and isolate. Alive in wonder, humility, and the recognition of mystery, the spirit is not static but a way of perceiving and engaging with the world. It enriches our experience of life by holding contradictions without resolving them into certainty. This ongoing dialogue between analysis and intuition characterizes the life of the spirit.

The soul, by contrast, is the still and infinitely deep well within us. In *Moby-Dick*, Melville writes: "From beneath his slouched hat Ahab dropped a tear into the sea; nor did all the Pacific contain such wealth as that one wee drop." The soul is the wealth in that tear. It is what endures, a place of reckoning and silence where we sense what is most fundamental in ourselves.

The soul is the ground of Being, a fundamental and non-transient stillness within us that is the source of meaning, love, and connection. It is always there, untouched, like the depth of the ocean, by whatever wind stirs the surface of our lives. It is available in and around every gesture, every word.

Yet it is not uncommon to live unaware of it, as we might be of the sea's depth and power while lying adrift on gentle waves.

When something alerts us that we are drifting, navigating half-asleep, without a sense of direction or connection to what is around us, we often respond by trying to uncover what seems hidden, hoping to achieve a higher state of awareness. This aspiration, while perhaps a necessary jolt in the journey of waking up, separate us from the immediacy of experience by striving for something that seems to be everywhere but where we are. If we keep the attention but shed the striving, realizing there is no hidden essence to uncover, what is eternal and immutable in us becomes apparent.

Let's go back to our question: *what characterizes the life of the spirit?* As I see it, the life of the spirit is not a state to master, it is a relaxing into being, a way of engaging with the world shaped by attention and by the presence we bring to the engagement. It is not achieved through force or ingenuity but through receptivity, through a willingness to allow meaning to emerge rather than imposing it. It thrives in the space between knowing and unknowing, in the awareness that certainty is often only a way of feeling our way in the dark. To live a life of the spirit is not to pursue transcendence but to inhabit the world more deeply, recognizing that what we seek is not elsewhere, but here—in the shifting light on the water, in the wind lifting the leaves, in the silence that falls over the riverbank. It is attunement to the rhythms of being.

To live fully might mean letting go of the need to overcome limits and instead seeing life as it unfolds, without judgment or expectation. Truth and love are not goals to be worked toward but arise naturally when the noise of seeking subsides. They exist not in reaching a higher state but in the clarity of a mind unburdened by its projections.

Although I'm attempting to say something about them, the life of the spirit and the nature of the soul resist explanations. To approach them requires reverence, imagination, and humility. Together—though they were never apart—they illuminate the human experience, revealing its depth, beauty, and mystery. The call to wholeness is not external, nor is it internal. It does not come from adding something we lack, nor is it something to find. It emerges in the absence of division, in the moment we stop searching, stop striving. Wholeness is not reached but recognized, not achieved but revealed, when the distance between what we are and what we seek collapses. In this space, life is no longer a journey to somewhere else but an unfolding presence, free of resistance and free of fear.

JH: Through the years, I have been repeatedly asked to define and differentiate these terms: *mind, spirit, psyche*, and *soul*. While there are many traditions with answers to these queries, many different ways of defining them, my definitions have been meant to serve functional understandings and embody how we might experience them in our lives. None of us know fully what these terms point to for they are energies, not entities that we isolate and put in a museum or under a microscope. But we also need operational words to help us talk about these energies and how they operate in our lives.

Perhaps it is prudent to remember the elemental axioms of general semantics. First of all, the map is not the territory. One of the most distressful moments in our lives occurs when, at mid-life for example, we arrive at a provisional, and perhaps achieved, sense of self and world. We have created relationship, work life, family, citizenship and so on, in service to the world of paradigm, instruction, and expectation in which we live. And then our outer world changes dramatically, a divorce occurs, loss of a significant relationship, a depression, whatever and we are suddenly adrift on the sea of uncertainty. The road map we were given, and perhaps trusted, no longer describes a recognizable terrain. Those moments are variously more than bumps in the road; they are crises, or dark nights of the soul. Not only are the guideposts missing, but one experiences a loss of meaning, purpose, direction.

In those difficult hours we turn to the resources of mind to try to figure things out, perhaps to revivify the old plan, if possible, or borrow someone else's plan, or, less commonly, wait with attentive patience till the next roadmap appears. We all know what the brain is, that marvelous organ that is able to compute so much so quickly. (Although one lawyer, seeking any possible argument in his failing case, actually asked a coroner on the witness stand, "Are you sure that the decedent was dead?" The physician replied, "Yes, especially since I had removed his brain.") But both anatomists and philosophers have wondered, if mind is an organ, what is mind, what creates the capacity even to reflect upon itself? It's the "ghost in the machine" as some more poetic minds have averred. Brain waves are physics and chemistry at work, but what is thinking, singing, creating? And we do not know. Those acts are epiphenomena, secondary activities of the primary neurological complexity. While we know more and more about the brain and its neural pathways, we are left with phenomenology and depth psychology to describe the conditions in which, the limitations of which, and the tendencies toward which mind functions. In short, the more we know, the less we know we do not know.

One thing each of us knows experientially is that when something confronts us, whether beauty or terror, evoking either a strong autonomous somatic and affective response, we feel the "quickening" of some energy within us we call the *spirit*. When the world in which we live is monochromatic, when the surges of life are blocked, we suffer a diminution, even oppression, of that energy. We may call that being dispirited. Being dispirited is not quite the same as being depressed though they are kissing cousins. When the agenda of the soul is blocked, the evocation of that energy we call the *soul* is drained.

I recall a client once who in his late seventies had lost his partner, his children had moved away, and he had no place where his former satisfying work could be practiced. He explained that he had gone to mixers, volunteered for a charity, and generally tried to keep in touch with outer life, including travel, but all had left him flat and hopeless. All of these "constructive strategies" were offered to him by magazines, and well-intentioned people around him, but depression nibbled at his ankles. All of these good, and conventional plans, were "oughts," perhaps oughts that had worked for others, but left him flat.

So, what I queried, was it that stirred your imagination when you were a child? What quickened the spirit? What did you look forward to exploring with enthusiasm? Immediately he replied, he loved to go where history had happened and trace its lingering numinosity. Whether it was a rural battlefield, a city where large events occurred, or places where history unfolded, something in him still stirred, embers flickered. What was missing for him was "permission" to take this childhood curiosity seriously. As a child, he was unable to travel, and as a conditioned adult he had "put away childish things." What I lobbied for in him was the recognition that the spirit was autonomous. We do not choose it; it manifests for us when we align our behaviors with the soul. *The spirit, in short, is the energy available to soul.* No matter how well-intentioned we are, no matter how productive we are, when the soul is not in accord we will find, as brother Hamlet did, "how stale and profitless is this world."

So it may be that we have to turn to this matter of soul, then.

Humans are those peculiar creatures that yearn to connect with something "missing." And so they go in search, always searching, always longing, never satisfied for very long. The terrible irony is that they search for what they are already carrying inside themselves all along—the soul.

The central fact of the post-modern world is that the link to the mysterious other, once mediated by tribal mythology and efficacious rituals, has eroded, leaving humans adrift, rudderless, and quite ill-tempered. Disconnected, they go in search of more or better sex, the latest shiny object, or, in some cases, attempt to revivify a link to the opaque gods, long after they have departed.

Pre-Socratic philosopher Heraclitus opined, "One will never discover the limits of soul, should one even traverse every road—so deep a measure does it possess." What we intuit and call "soul" is a mystery. We know very little about it. But it is tangibly real. The word *psyche* is the Greek word for soul. It comes from two etymological sources. First is the verb *psychein,* "to breathe." It's that life force that moves through us; that inspiration, respiration, the breath of the invisible energy that courses through the body and animates it, ensouls it. Second, it is related to the image of the butterfly—something that transforms from the pupae over time into something beautiful. It's elusive; you can't quite get your hand on it; it flits away and yet is stunning to behold. These two examples of the primal, threads of the ancient mythopoetic imagination sought to intimate the mystery of the psyche by identifying something we know to serve as simulacrum of, or arrow pointing toward, what we experience but do not know.

Along with many others in analysis, I learned to honor the world of dreams, of active imagination, and to begin to ask questions such as, "But what is that choice in service to inside?" A simple enough question, but it begins the forensic deepening. The problem with the unconscious is that it is unconscious. Recently, while in the hospital, I was asked by a nurse what I did for a living. "How does that work differ from ordinary psychology?" she asked. "Well, for one thing, we try to evoke a conversation with the unconscious." She thought awhile and replied, "Oh, I get it, you work with folks in a coma." The more I reflected on her comment, the more sense it made for all of us most of the time are in altered states, that is to say, driven by fears, responding to life's challenges with routinized and reflexive behaviors, and largely unaware of the vast psychodramas coursing beneath the surface of things. Even if popular culture itself is a vast panoply of distractions from the life of the soul, there are many who know something vital is missing in all that flash, flair, and razzmatazz.

We all recall Jung's observation that most of our problems stem from being separated from our instincts. As our journey begins in utter powerlessness and dependency upon those whom fate has assigned to us, we survive as creatures of adaptation. Over time, repeated on a daily basis, these adaptations become reflexive, even autonomous responses to the challenges that arise from our families and our assigned culture. No wonder one grows a stranger to oneself. No wonder we become our own worst enemy. We even cling to our maladaptive behaviors for they are the boat that brought us this far. Sometimes, the natural maturational process allows us to outgrow the childhood fears and epiphenomenal behaviors, but many times they become institutionalized within us as shadow governments. Often it takes a crisis, a loss of energy, or a set of troubling consequences that oblige us to stop and finally settle accounts, perhaps start therapy, perhaps tough it out on one's own.

Sooner or later each of us is obliged to traverse the savannahs of suffering. Sooner or later evil makes its way into our lives, along with loss, defeat, and the seductive temptations of lassitude and avoidance. But even the darkest of hours is part of the richness of this journey we call our lives. No matter what happens to us "out there," so much more is asked of us from within. Sustaining the energy, the focus, the fierce commitment to growth and learning is difficult but critical to the depth and dignity of our journey. For each of us, the turn of the wheel of time brings us over and over to the question: "*How* shall you live in the face of this situation over which you, seemingly, have no control?" This question personalizes the challenge to us directly. One remembers the 1950s letter of Jung to Olga Fröbe-Kapteyn in which he said the opus of individuation consists of three parts, of which psychology can only help with the first stage: insight. Then, he said, come the moral qualities of the individual: courage to face whatever must be faced, and persistence, endurance over time until one has lived into a different place.

I am also always reminded of Jung's query: "What supports you when nothing supports you?" Sooner or later, the constructed edifice of the false self will erode, even collapse, and then one enters the dark night of the soul. Will one, in all that intimidating darkness, find even a scintilla of light that leads one through and out of the dark forest? If we find, hold onto, and risk that glimmer of light, then we know we carry something that transcends the ordinary ego limitations that bind us to the dreary cycle of repetition. Such a person knows from then on that she or he is never alone in one's aloneness, that one is never bereft of support within, and that if we simply try to do the next right thing as we believe it to be right, something within will rise and support us. In the vast star-flung sea of the universe, the human soul has a resilience and a buoyancy that one does not know.... Until one knows it. As I noted before, poet Emily Dickinson put it in an aphorism: "The sailor cannot see the north, but knows the needle can." Her 1863 insight reminds us that when we venture forth on the high seas of uncertain voyage, we must remember to bring and to trust the compass within that tells us the true north of the soul.

A friend and colleague recently dreamed that she was on a raft on the open seas, and a large form emerged from the depths, and she found herself poised over a beluga whale, which carries her and her craft: "As it moves under me, I roll with it knowing somewhere inside that I have to ride the momentum, knowing it is the whale, not I, who is in charge. It is a marvelous ride, and I smile as it then swims away."

Don't we all want to know more about those large forms that roll beneath the surface of our lives? Don't we all want to experience the full joy and terror of that ride? Don't we all want to engage what carries us through this journey we call our life?

When we ask, "from whence comes those guiding dreams," we cannot say. Yet, they are palpably present, and unmistakably our dreams. So what has produced them within us? (If we reach eighty years of age, we will have dreamt for six of them.) Not sleeping, per se, but dreaming. Nature does not waste energy. Yes, those dreams are processing the debris and detritus of daily life, but if we attend their imagery, we find much more. We find that some "intelligence" within knows us better than we know ourselves.

Further, we track the autonomy of our feeling function that not only discharges neurologically but has a qualitative analysis to offer from the standpoint of that inner knowing. Additionally, we learn that our symptoms rise to alert us, caution us, redirect us according to an agenda that is not always comforting to the ego but is nevertheless advancing the agenda of soul. When we learn to dialogue with these symptoms, we move to a deeper conversation than is capable through the conscious life on its own.

Most of all, the inner "genius," from the Latin for tutelary spirit, our link to the soul, informs us what is meaningful to us, or not. Disconnects from meaning are the chief source of human suffering. Life will bring suffering sooner or later, but it is far worse when we suffer without meaning, but enriching when we know the meaning of our suffering, and the tasks which it asks of us.

Sociologist Zygmunt Baumann posited that as recently as the late nineteenth century, the idea of "progress" animated the Western world—a better society, better health and longevity, international peace, and strength through the cultivation of personal character. Today, he asserted, it is change for the sake of change that drives our lives. Thus we become the "hungry ghosts," as the indigenous tribes of America described. Coming, devouring, moving on, and repeating the process incessantly. Driven by emptiness, we fill ourselves with products, distractions, and the latest shiny thing or fad.

I have spent the last sixty years in education, teaching either the humanities or the principles and practices of analytic psychology. For all that effort, I cannot say that we have improved our society for it seems more and more fractured, disquieted, and antagonistic. But I think it fair and accurate to say that the lives of certain individuals are better able to handle this time of fracture and discord. Helping people find their internal compass remains one tool that supports individuals in holding to their inner guide in transitory times. The advent of the modern internet, the Zoom-world, means that more and more of those at distance, or those disadvantaged, might access this source of developmental encouragement. At the same time, the same venues are flush with hate-filled ideologies and a thousand seductions of the spirit. All we can do, is what we can do, and when we go to bed at night, believe that it might make some small difference.

In the end, the summons of life comes down to recovering for ourselves, individually and collectively, a relationship to what we are calling "soul." To reiterate, something inside of each of us is guiding us and knows what is best for us in the face of the troubles and distempers of this journey. The more we are aligned with that purpose, the more we are rewarded with a sense of purpose. Our goal is not to be happy, for happiness is contextual, and transitory. Our goal is to find the meaning in our lives no matter what the context.

I remain deeply moved by a letter I read from Pastor Dietrich Bonhoeffer. He was safe in America teaching when the Hitlerian thugs took over his country. He felt called to leave his safety and return to oppose them. Ultimately, though a pacifist, he leant support to the plan to assassinate Hitler, believing that political decapitation was the only way to end the mass suffering. While in prison, awaiting his own execution, he asked himself: is this place the will of God? He concluded no, it is the will of humans. But, his task, he knew, was to find the will of his God for him in that terrible place, and to live it as best he could. In so doing we see a model of the individuation process. We do not individuate by becoming narcissistically driven individuals, nor by having a good time for the sake of good time. We individuate by discerning over time what is worthy of our service, and by serving it. Then we are flushed with meaning, and an inner sense of the rightness of our choices. No matter how conscientious we have been hitherto, no matter how faithfully we followed the well-intentioned directions of others, no matter how "successful" we have been in the eyes of the world, if we have not served something larger, we will have served something too small for the soul.

12

What do you think the numinous is?
What engages your spirit?
Take one painting and talk about how and why it moves you.

The lamps are different,
But the Light is the same.

Rumi

JH: Jung's psychiatric career began in the Burghölzli Hospital that stands still as the Kantonal Hospital of Zürich. In those pioneer days, where everything was being explored for the first time, reconsidered, relabeled, redefined, Jung was steeped in the development of the etiology, diagnosis, treatment plan paradigm that prevails to this day. But in later years, he said that he had grown less interested in psychopathy than in the approach to the numinous. In fact, he concluded that it only through the approach to the numinous that we can talk about healing. I use the word "healing," rather than curing, because many situations cannot be cured, but they may be healed. Healing occurs when the person moves from the confines of the dilemma, the presenting situation, to a much larger reframing. In other words, we may not "solve" psychopathy, but we may outgrow it, or find its purpose or meaning in our lives.

We get the concept "numinous" from the 1917 work by Rudolf Otto titled *The Idea of the Holy*. The word itself comes from a Latin verb "to nod or beckon." That is, something beckons, touches us, stirs a response.

Two people enter a gallery or art museum and stand before various canvases daubed with pigments. One is touched, one indifferent. Which one of them is "right?" One experiences the painting through a thoughtful analysis. Another feels a deep resonance that does not lend itself to discursive language. Another is swarmed with a mood state, vague but compelling. Something in that surface daubed with pigment has the power, mysterious power, to stir that deep resonance, re-sonance, that resounding within by thrumming the chords of the unconscious. Someone else is stirred to martial spirit by a marching band, but another is left indifferent until flushed with emotion having heard some Delta blues.

As I reported elsewhere, during my analytic training days in Switzerland, I was a frequent visitor to the city Kunsthaus, or Municipal Art Gallery. Invariably I found myself drawn to an ancient Roman statue of the slain satyr Masyras. Masyras found a flute, and in his inflation, challenged Apollo, god of music among other things, to a contest. It is not good for one's resume to challenge a god. Having lost the contest to the god, Masyras is flayed alive in a kind of pre-Christian crucifixion. When the same image as the statue occurred in my dreams, I realized that I was being moved by some strange energy. Later, I came to realize that that statue was outwardly embodying for me the flaying of the hubris of thinking I knew who I was or what I was really doing. Similarly, for many years I was drawn to Rilke's short lyric titled

"On the Archaic Torso of Apollo." Here is my loose translation of that sonnet, but faithful, I believe, to the spirit of the poem.

> We cannot fathom his marvelous head
> From which the luminous eyes bulge.
> But that body radiates like a candelabra
> And his contained glance glows.
>
> Otherwise the curving breast
> Might not dazzle you nor might
> The telluric power of generativity
> Arc into the dark genitalia.
>
> Otherwise this ancient stone
> Would leave you untouched
> Like a wild beast's fur
>
> Instead of radiating like a star.
> You who watch here, are being watched:
> You must change your life!

At first reading that last line seems like a non sequitur, and then it comes to one as an instant metanoia such as what must have gripped the observer of the statue. In some distant land, some antique epoch, the spirit of an unknown sculptor moved through his limbs and shaped that dead matter, animated that inert stone, bringing it to life. Its numinosity confronts the viewer and apparently calls the observer to an accounting. In the face of such largeness, it challenges, how can you remain comfortable in your smallness? How can you remain at ease in your old dispensation, your familiar constraining frame? You must change your life! When we are in the presence of the numinous, something sees through us, and calls all we are into an accounting.

Sometimes the numinous is invested in a person. "Was this," Christopher Marlowe questions, "the face that launched a thousand ships, / and burned the topless towers of Ilium?" Sometimes the numinous is experienced in nature. Sometimes in art. One such moment occurred to me when, as a sophomore in college, I slipped away from a tour group seeing The Big Apple for the first time to visit two shrines of which I was in awe: Yankee Stadium and the Museum of Modern Art. In the one temple I saw that God with feet of clay, Mickey Mantle, and in that other temple of visionary experiences that contained so many works I grew to cherish, one painting touched me and remains a favorite to this day sixty-five years later. It is Pavel Tchechelitchew's "Hide and Seek."

Pavel Fyodorovich Tchelitchew (1898-1957) was a Russian surrealist painter whose family left Russia at the time of the 1917 revolution. He later lived in Paris and moved to New York in 1934. The painting "Hide and Seek" was painted between 1934-42 and has long been the property of the Museum of Modern Art.

That it continues to resonate after so many years intimates that it carries the numinous energy, at least for me. As such it lies beyond discursive thinking, and ordinary articulation, so my reflections here are not meant to be interpretations. This work needs no interpretation; it is, rather, an experience, inexplicable and compelling.

Digital Image © The Museum of Modern Art/Licensed by SCALA / Art Resource, NY
Artist: Tchelitchew, Pavel (1898-1957)
Description: Hide-and-Seek. Derby, Vermont and New York, June 1940 - June 1942. Oil on canvas, 6' 6 1/2" x 7' 3/4" (199.3 x 215.3 cm). Mrs. Simon Guggenheim Fund.

The oils are expressionistic, stunning, and the style surrealistic. Surrealism was perhaps the most notable of those schools of art to rise out of the impact of psychoanalysis in the early twentieth century. Freud's insights into the workings of the unconscious, its displacement, its distortions, its meta-symbolic language which we all know from our dreams, provided not only a platform for understanding but a commentary on daily life. If anything was surreal it was contemporary events. The most "civilized" nations on the planet were tearing each other to pieces in such slaughterhouses as

Verdun, Passchendaele, and the Ardennes. To paraphrase Joyce's spokesman Stephen Daedalus, history is a living nightmare from which it is so difficult to awake.

There is an old Zen koan that informs that we are all looking for the face we had before the world was made, that is, for our archetypal identity which exists before our individual births and journeys. To know who we are, to connect with that timeless part of ourselves is, whether conscious or not, a life-long journey. When Yeats looks at our various stages of life, various identities in "Among School Children," he intuits that we are both origin and entelechy, and all the stages in between. Analogizing the one amid the many via the metaphor of the chestnut tree, he asks are we the leaf, the blossom, or the bole, or rather all of the above, an archetypal energy expressing itself through an unfolding differentiation just as it does in all of our separate lives. Given that, an artist, as a visitor to the depths within, may return to the surface, like Orpheus, with an image makes this universal process which we all embody available to consciousness. One of the surrealist painter/poets, Paul Eluard, is thought to have said, "There is another world, and it is in this one." I consider that sentence also a description of psychoanalytic work, the hermetic explorations of how the visible and invisible worlds meet, touch, and inform each other.

A number of years ago, my son Timothy introduced me to the Santa Fe artist Frank Howell who was half Anglo, half Sioux. We visited his studio and discussed his capacity to reach below the individual manifestation and tap into the archetypal energy field. His surrealistic work evokes something timeless in the indigenous spirits who haunt that environment and have proved very resonant for the public. He said to me that he could not understand how strangers could come to his studio, stand before a painting, and weep, saying that it reminded them of their grandparent. "Why would they say that?" he asked. "I don't know their grandparent." Like many artists, though not my writing companion in this book, he was a vehicle for energies, but could not step out of them and reflect upon from whence they came. I referenced the archetypal field that he, as an artist could visit, portray, and return, but it didn't seem to make any sense to him.

I bought his hand painted lithograph, "Lakota Dancer," and it hangs ten feet from me now.

Frank Howell "Lakota Dancer."

If the reader concludes from these two examples alone, "Lakota Dancer" and "Hide and Seek," that I prefer symbolic and surrealistic painting over other forms such as natural scenes, as in Corot, or realistic portraits by such as David, they are correct. While I admire those and many other schools of art for their technical skills, I do not experience the numinous in them. That does not, of course, mean that I do not see something in them the reader might, it simply reminds us that what is numinous for one person is not for another. *De gustibus, non disputatum est.*

But back to "Hide and Seek." Most readers will have played the game "hide and seek" in childhood. And while an exercise in childhood play, it also embodies our life-long search for our personal identities, and intuitive sense that our particular lives are part of some trans-personal, trans-historic movements. (As an old Chippewa musing had it, "I spend my life in all my little worries and all the while I am carried by great winds across the sky.")

The shape of the tree itself replicates a human hand seeking purchase on the mystery, the recondite. The tree is itself is an archetypal image: grounded in the Great Mother earth, its arms reach toward the spirit world. Its roots branch out into the fructifying loam that nurtures even as its arms differentiate and diversify in a thousand individuating arms. It, too, goes through transmogrification from seed to a great presence against the sky. As Yeats concluded in "Among School Children," it is unity amid diversity. Additionally, we see, as if in a hologram, how the smallest cluster of energy, arranged in this material form for a short while, contains the fractal elements of the whole, and in the whole the trillion variants are contained. Moreover, the arterial system of the eyes, reminiscent of Borges's "The Garden of Forking Paths," serve as amniotic sacs for the possible variant next to it. And through all, the arteries link one to the bloodweb lacing the walls of the great womb of nature, from whence may emerge the many possibles. Has there ever been a single painting that depicted the mystery of created life so profoundly as "Hide and Seek"?

The images of the fetal variants that feed into the uniqueness of the individual remind us we carry the whole history of humanity in our DNA. In us, each of us, the stardust that we carry antedates the planets themselves, and yet embody in the Joe or Susan we know in the other room. In John Barth's short story, based on an archetype "The Night Sea Journey," we enter the thoughts of a single sperm as it survives the perilous journey to homecoming. Driven by desire, the protagonist is the one among the many to reach the ovum, and carry on the latest chapter in an old, old story. With each new child, singing "love's old sweet song," the ancient renews itself.

In response to the question "what do you seek," the answer has to be coming home to oneself, in the timeless sense of that question. And as we seek, something is seeking us. From that prospective meeting one may well experience the possibility of healing the deep estrangement our time has exacted of us, the countless adaptations necessary to fit in, or protect ourselves. As poet Friedrich Hölderlin once wrote, that which we seek is near and already coming to meet us. Dream work, art, meditation, and such resonant moments are our vehicles for healing the painful splits within and coming home to ourselves once more. Only then will this foreign land we all wander become our blessed home.

EMC: One of the most recognized passages in literature comes from *Swann's Way*, the first volume of Marcel Proust's *In Search of Lost Time*. The narrator, lifting a madeleine to his mouth, is suddenly overcome, and the past arrives whole, indistinguishable from the present.

This is one form of the numinous. The manner in which something ordinary brings forth what lies beneath the surface of perception. A recognition of what has always been there, waiting for a crack in awareness or time to make itself known. A madeleine touches the tongue and the self opens to and thereby joins something boundless, the elasticity of time:

> a shudder ran through my whole body, and I stopped, intent upon the extraordinary changes that were taking place. An exquisite pleasure had invaded my senses, but individual, detached, with no suggestion of its origin. And at once the vicissitudes of life had become indifferent to me, its disasters innocuous, its brevity illusory—this new sensation having had on me the effect which love has of filling me with a precious essence; or rather this essence was not in me, it was myself.

We live between presence and absence, between what appears and what fades. Every experience carries its opposite, as crest carries trough. Yet we often forget this unity. We look before and after, measuring what has been and what might come, and in doing so, overlook the harmony unfolding within us—the adjustments, rhythms, and responses that keep us alive without our knowing. Our true self is not this restless stream of thought but the stillness beneath it. When we lose sight of that stillness, we begin to live through abstractions, mistaking plans, numbers, and words for life itself. We postpone living for a future that never arrives, believing that meaning will come later. To be fully present is to enter the moment where opposites meet, where self and world are no longer divided. It is there, in that instant of undivided being, that the numinous becomes perceptible.

Proust's madeleine is often cited as a moment of nostalgia, but, to me, it is something else. Time, for a moment, ceases to move forward. What had seemed lost is not only present again but inseparable from and reshaping of the self. This is not simply the retrieval of a memory but an undoing of time itself, a moment in which past and present collapse into a single experience of being. The numinous, in this sense, does not announce itself through revelation but through recognition. It is the sudden realization that nothing essential has ever been lost.

Ralph Waldo Emerson saw this same opening, not in memory, but in nature. For him, the numinous was a force that moved through all things, waiting to be encountered by those who were attentive enough. Emerson wrote of the moments when the self dissolves into a greater unity, when the edges of identity blur, and something larger moves through us. In *Nature*, he describes a vision where the ordinary world suddenly reveals its hidden immensity, and what had seemed separate discloses its belonging to a single, living whole:

> The greatest homage we can pay to truth is to use it. In the woods, we return to reason and faith. There I feel that nothing can befall me in life,—no disgrace, no calamity (leaving me my eyes), which nature cannot repair. Standing on the bare ground—my head bathed by the blithe air and uplifted into infinite space—all mean egotism vanishes. I become a transparent eyeball; I am nothing; I see all; the currents of the Universal Being circulate through me; I am part and parcel of God.

His was not an intellectual revelation but an experience where the boundaries of self give way to something larger. He saw the numinous as something embedded in the fabric of the world, not confined to religious doctrine but available to anyone who approached the world with reverence. It came through an openness of being, an ability to see without imposing. In *The Over-Soul*, he wrote of an eternal presence, a stillness beneath the surface of life, something that binds all things together:

> We live in succession, in division, in parts, in particles. Meantime within man is the soul

> of the whole; the wise silence; the universal beauty, to which every part and particle is equally related, the eternal ONE. And this deep power in which we exist and whose beatitude is all accessible to us, is not only self-sufficing and perfect in every hour, but the act of seeing and the thing seen, the seer and the spectacle, the subject and the object, are one. We see the world piece by piece, as the sun, the moon, the animal, the tree; but the whole, of which these are shining parts, is the soul.

This presence, he believed, was immediate, available, woven into the world itself. To experience it required shedding the distractions of ambition, of self-importance, of the noise that dulls our capacity to perceive. It required solitude, attentiveness, the willingness to be shaped rather than to control. For Emerson, the numinous was not an escape but a deeper inhabiting of reality. An intensified attention.

What engages my spirit is whatever sharpens that attention. The luminous whitecaps in the sea at night. The first light of morning. The hush before a storm. The charged air in an old room. The way moonlight alters the swing set in my yard. The scent of vermouth bringing me back to my grandfather's dining room in Cuba. The moment when a painting stands apart from me and whispers a secret. The childhood photograph of my daughter saying with her eyes to the current me, "You do not exist for me." The loud rumbling of a crashing wave. A breeze rustling the leaves of a tree. The exactness of a gesture, understood without words. The pull between solitude and connection, between what is known and what is beyond reach. More than impressions, these are thresholds to the vast unseen, drawing us beyond the edges of our lives.

Rainer Maria Rilke in the poem, "Go to the Limits of Your Longing," from *The Book of Hours: Love Poems to God*, writes:

> God speaks to each of us as he makes us,
> then walks with us silently out of the night.
>
> These are the words we dimly hear:
>
> You, sent out beyond your recall,
> go to the limits of your longing.
> Embody me.
>
> Flare up like a flame
> and make big shadows I can move in.
>
> Let everything happen to you: beauty and terror.
> Just keep going. No feeling is final.
> Don't let yourself lose me.
>
> Nearby is the country they call life.
> You will know it by its seriousness.
>
> Give me your hand.

To go to the limits of our longing, to extend a hand to that which walks with us silently out of the night, requires trust. Somewhat like Rilke, I recognize a presence that is both within and beyond, something that must be continually rediscovered. Being trained as a physicist, it is natural for me to think that the reality we see and touch is not everything. It is only what we can apprehend through the systems, sensors, and degrees of awareness we possess. While we cannot easily change our senses, we can expand our awareness, and through that expansion begin to apprehend, or at least sense, aspects of reality that are not normally available to us. The materialist understanding of the world falls short, not only of what many of us experience, but also of what physics knows. The idea that a mechanistic system, whether scientific or social, offers the truest picture of reality overlooks much: the discoveries of science itself, the findings of psychedelic research, and our own direct experience. In physics, ultimate reality bears little resemblance to what we perceive. The table beneath my hand feels solid and certain, but that is not its fundamental nature. It is only the macroscopic impression my senses register in this moment. Look deeper, and the table dissolves into field fluctuations, delocalized energy, and the vanishing of clear separations between things that seem, for now, distinct. Physics teaches us that there is a deeper order that is not fixed but emergent, relational, and in constant transformation. Space itself is not empty but a dynamic medium, shaped by unseen structures that give rise to everything we perceive. What seems solid, separate, or defined is, at its most fundamental level, fluid and interconnected, more process than thing.

Our ways of knowing are themselves part of this unfolding, never capturing the whole but approaching it through intuition, deep attention, contemplation, and, most broadly, in those experiences we describe as the numinous. If physics dismantles the illusion of solidity, the numinous dismantles the illusion of control. It does not arrive through system or prediction but unbidden, in moments that pierce through the ordinary—through beauty, through grief, through a small rupture in meaning. It bypasses rational understanding and evokes awe, fear, or connection.

A sense of the numinous reminds us that nothing belongs to us, that everything is passing through. That to love is to bear the weight of impermanence without turning away. It breaks apart many of our plans and anything else that is too rigid in ourselves, leaving us exposed and reshaping the self from within.

While there is no guaranteed method for encountering the numinous, it sometimes reveals itself in an art experience, and it is this connection between the two that I want to explore before turning to my response to a specific painting.

The Rothko Chapel is a blocky building in Houston constructed primarily of poured-in-place concrete. The interior is lit with dim, shifting natural light filtering from an overhead skylight, its unadorned gray walls enclosing fourteen monumental paintings by Mark Rothko in deep hues of black, maroon, and purple. There are accounts of people sitting in that room and weeping without knowing why. Rothko once said he wanted his paintings to "remove the veil from our eyes," to bring the viewer into direct confrontation with something beyond the self. He described the paintings as thresholds—spaces where the visible and invisible meet. The poet John Taggart wrote about sitting in front of one of those dark paintings and feeling the boundaries between himself and the painting dissolve, as if the work absorbed him, drawing him into an awareness of time slowing, of silence deepening, of being in the presence of something that resisted explanation but demanded total attention.

People have had similar experiences with other immersive spaces, like Claude Monet's *Water Lilies* at the Musée de l'Orangerie in Paris or Michelangelo's Sistine Chapel in Rome. But the numinous can also emerge in the encounter with a single work. Many paintings, sculptures, photographs, and tapestries have brought me to an experience of an unseen presence, evoking awe, mystery, and a sense of something immense beyond my grasp: Leonardo's *Virgin of the Rocks*, Rembrandt's late self-portraits, Manet's *A Bundle of Asparagus*, almost every painting by Vincent Van Gogh or Forrest Bess. Recently, I had a powerful encounter with the numinous brought about by a small painting by the seventeenth-century Spanish artist Diego Velázquez.

I had the opportunity to create a project for the Hispanic Society in New York that included an installation of my work and one painting by Velázquez—*Portrait of a Little Girl* (ca. 1638–42). This portrait is not a grand painting like *Las Meninas*. It is small, about 20 × 16 inches, among his most intimate and compelling works, and it stands apart in his body of work as one of only two images of non-royal children and the only one in which the subject is alone. The identity of the girl, perhaps six to eight years old, remains unknown. Her serious expression, softened by the slightest hint of a smile, suggests familiarity—perhaps a relative, possibly a granddaughter, as some scholars have proposed. Regardless of who she was, the painting is immensely powerful.

Diego Velázquez, *Portrait of a Little Girl*, ca. 1638-1642.
Courtesy of the Hispanic Society of America, New York.

I have known this little girl since I was her age. My mother had wrapped my first-grade notebook with a magazine illustration of the painting. For me, she was not a work of art but a companion, a confidant. I got to know her well over a year of dictation and grammar, and, fortunately, my grandmother saved the notebook, so I was able to include it in the exhibition. The image is very moving, even in reproduction, but a painting is not the same as a magazine illustration. I had never seen it in real life until the day of the installation. I walked into the room, ignored my work, and went straight to the Velázquez.

It was hung so that her eyes were slightly lower than mine. The composition was even simpler in real life, freed from the distracting orange tone of the old varnish. It glowed, but its power came in part from its restraint, something for which the artist was known. He captured the essence of the girl with brief gestures, a loose movement of his brush—the delicate light across her face, the understated shine in her dark hair, the faint orange-pink of her lips.

Was she about to smile or about to speak? It doesn't matter. Those are only superficial stories. Her mouth resisted stories or explanations. It was alive, though not like your mouth or mine—more than ours, truer. And her eyes. Browner than I had thought, except for the bright speck of light at the upper edge of her pupil, and the softer light traveling through the lens and emerging, dimly, at the boundary between the dark iris and the whitish sclera. Those eyes looked at me across four hundred years and saw me better than

I could see myself. She knew my secrets, but remained a mystery to me. Her nose seemed to breathe the air of both the room where Velázquez painted her and the one where I stood. And in what room was she painted? We don't know. She lives in a rectangle of umber. In the painting, she was more self-possessed, more composed, more distant than the approachable confidant she had been on the cover of my notebook.

I couldn't understand what I was seeing. She was a painting. But she was also alive in 2024, and I was certain she would be alive past my death. She was timeless, holding all the wisdom of four centuries. No—of all time.

As I drew closer to her face, her elusiveness grew, and, paradoxically, the painting revealed its truth with greater clarity. Was I sensing Velázquez or the spirit of the little girl? Or maybe I was feeling the essence of painting? Or the ineffable nature of time? Or myself—but not myself as I knew me—something more distilled, more elemental? Sometimes I settled on one of these. Other times, I felt that they were all in there.

It was the numinous I was experiencing. The painting opened a vastness that was neither in time nor in space, but in the fundamental nature of existence from which both arise. It was vast, and I could feel myself being swallowed by it, and just when I thought I might not return, I felt I was that same vastness. The little girl and I were one, something more elemental than the most basic reality I had encountered in physics. Each time I stepped back from the painting, I felt changed by the encounter, yet when I tried to understand how, I couldn't explain it. There were two of me: one before seeing the painting, and one after.

At the opening of my exhibition, my friend Marty and I looked at it together. We marveled at the way the lips were painted and commented on the loosely sketched dress. We traced her skin with our eyes, telling each other to look at this or that detail. We kept talking, but our words seemed to be only bubbles rising from a deep, secret ocean we were part of, one we could neither understand nor measure, though we could feel the pressure that vastness exerted on us.

13

What is meaning and purpose? How has your understanding of meaning and purpose evolved over time, and what experiences have most influenced this evolution?

This is how he grows; by being defeated, decisively,
By ever-larger things.

R. M. Rilke

EMC: My father often recounted the story of an exchange between us when I was about three years old. I had been walking, he told me, under the casuarina pines of the small Caribbean beach town where I spent part of my childhood, and had gathered a handful of the little pine cones that had fallen to the ground when he found me. Seeing him, I gave him the casuarina bounty, and my father was moved by the gift. "You gave me all you had," he told me many times. Probably five or six pine cones about the size of small grapes—that was my gift. They were not going to be planted or eaten. Their meaning for my father was not in their use, but in what they represented to him, and, eventually, to me. It wasn't the pine cones that mattered but the gesture, and the way it was received. For him, that handful of spiky cones became a symbol of love, trust, and generosity.

How significant is that meaning? Significant enough to be spoken about often by my father, and for me to make sculptures and paintings around an exchange that I don't remember, and to tell you about it here. The meaning that an event, object, gesture, relationship, memory or place has and will have is often not understood immediately, nor is that understanding independent of everything else. The meaning that gift has now is not only informed by a moment long ago in a country we left behind, but by the life we have lived and what we have learned along the way, including the recognition of the limited time we have with those we love.

Meaning is not a fixed entity. I find it helpful to think of it as an energy containing emotional, intellectual, and spiritual information, constantly fluctuating within the vessel that holds it. A memory can feel almost meaningless until, one day, resonating in the internal space created by a walk in the forest or the smell of a familiar soup, it radiates meaning so brightly that everything around it is illuminated in a new way. Conversely, something that once felt deeply meaningful can lose its radiance.

For me, the meaning of the pine cones shifted depending on the relationship between my father and me. During my adolescence and early twenties, when distance and conflict lingered between us, the pine cones felt like the most meaningful thing we had shared. Now, many years later, with life having softened old resentments and added nuance to what we once thought we understood, my father's loving appreciation of my pine cones feels like the true gift. I see it now as just one of many meaningful moments between us.

Like all energies, meaning responds to how it is observed and contained. The meaning of an event, object, gesture, relationship, memory, or place depends on who holds it and how that holding is shared. Something can become meaningful because more than one person is invested in it. For example, the meaning of the massive fires in Los Angeles in January 2025 differs for those of us who live in the city. Yet, part of the fire's significance lies in the shared experience of communal misery, fear, and loss. In the case of my father and me, although our reasons were not the same, we shared, for about fifty years, the belief that the pine cones were meaningful. That shared acknowledgment was part of what made the event so significant. A few years ago, my father's Alzheimer's took most of his memories. Now, I carry the meaning of that event for both of us, but some part of it—the part that came from the bond of sharing it—has changed, and maybe is lost.

Meaning weaves together the fragments of ourselves and the world into something whole, and more than anything else, it is what helps us bear challenges and allows us to find purpose in a life that comes without instruction manuals or enough time to wander aimlessly. Purpose, on the other hand, is the sense of direction that guides our actions. It offers a reason for being that organizes and motivates how we live. I used to think of purpose as a process of aligning with one's authentic self. Now, I think it not only relies on an inner journey or a quest for self-alignment, but also emerges from an ongoing relationship with the world around us. It is shaped by how we pay attention to life's fullness and mysteries, as well as the connections that bind us to others and to living itself.

In considering meaning and purpose at the moment of this writing, it seems important to recognize that we are on the brink of a crisis of purpose unlike any other in human history—one driven not by scarcity or survival but by the displacement of human effort itself. The accelerating presence of artificial intelligence will inevitably disrupt our long-standing frameworks for purpose, not just in how we work but in how we define ourselves within a world where human contribution is no longer required in many of the ways we once took for granted. When machines take over not only routine tasks but also creative, analytical, and decision-making roles, the question of what remains distinctly human will become more urgent than ever. Many of the activities that have historically provided people with meaning—building, problem-solving, teaching, even creative projects—will no longer be necessary in the same way. For some, this shift may offer new freedoms, a release from the burdens of obligation, and an opportunity to engage in pursuits that were once impractical. But for many, the disappearance of work as a central structure of life will provoke a crisis, forcing us to confront purpose beyond productivity. Without the scaffolding of professional identity, financial necessity, or externally imposed roles, which many equate with purpose, what will become of meaning and our sense of direction? Will purpose become something more fluid, shaped by curiosity, relationships, and deeper forms of engagement, or will it become an increasingly elusive ideal—a historical artifact or something to be manufactured in the absence of real necessity? The challenge will be learning how to cultivate meaning in a world where meaning is no longer assigned by function, where our role is not given but must be continually rediscovered. As artificial intelligence transforms not only our tasks but our sense of being needed, the ability to find purpose beyond utility may become one of the defining struggles of this era.

Yet even now, before this transformation fully takes hold, we can see how purpose resists simple definitions. In our slogan-oriented society, it's often assumed that purpose should be something we can articulate in words. But the more we learn to trust our intuitions and the subtle messages the inner and outer world are constantly sending us, the harder, less useful, and more prone to self-deception it becomes to reduce purpose to a mission statement. We tend to associate purpose with certainty, but purpose is less about certainty and more about immersing ourselves in the flow of life's complexity and embracing the tension between the known and the unknown, the inner and the outer, the self and the greater whole. Purpose is an evolving experience of being present within the unfolding of life, rather than a mandate or a goal to be achieved, as is often the case with drive.

It's easy to confuse purpose and drive. Drive propels us forward, often fueled by a compulsion to achieve, produce, and check off milestones. Drive thrives on measurable outcomes—promotion, recognition, personal optimization—but it can move us through life without asking why, blinding us to whether the direction we're heading holds any real significance. Without purpose, drive risks becoming aimless or even destructive, leaving us untethered and disconnected from what truly matters. Purpose, in contrast, gives direction and depth to our efforts, connecting them to something meaningful and enduring. It is not about doing more but about having a sense of why we do anything at all.

When we are driven without purpose, we become untethered. The energy of drive keeps us moving, but rarely rewards us with meaning. We chase success, visibility, or self-improvement for their own sake, mistaking motion for meaning. Purpose connects us to something beyond the chase or our ambition. It suggests that we slow down and look inward to consider what aligns with ourselves and how we can engage with the world in meaningful ways. It is less about reaching an endpoint or a certain status and more about the relationships we build, the values we hold, and the ways we live in alignment with what matters to us. Where drive can scatter us, purpose gathers us into a life that feels coherent, full, and true.

Life offers no intrinsic purpose, but this absence is not a loss. It is an opening, a chance to craft our own values and affirm life on our own terms. Purpose is created and fueled by the energy of meaning, which is shaped from the chaos and uncertainty of existence, using the raw material of our experiences, choices, and connections. Together, meaning and purpose form the framework through which we navigate life, helping us make sense of our experiences and align our actions with what we hold valuable. While meaning often arises from reflection on the "why" of our lives, purpose focuses on the "what" we do with it.

In *Man's Search for Meaning*, Viktor Frankl helps us understand the interplay and distinctions between meaning, purpose, and drive. In the concentration camps, meaning served as Frankl's foundation as something created through attention and interpretation, imbuing life's acts, gestures, and circumstances with significance. Frankl found meaning not by denying the horrors of his experience but by choosing to see his endurance as an act of bearing witness and contributing to others' understanding of resilience and hope. It was in this act of choosing that meaning began to take shape. By assigning significance to his suffering, he found justification to keep living.

While meaning arises from our engagement with life as it is, purpose provides a sense of where we are headed and why. For Frankl, purpose was not something handed down but created through individual choice. His purpose was not merely survival, though survival is always a critical component of purpose, but the pursuit of meaning through love, responsibility, and the defiant assertion of human freedom in the face of suffering. Even in the harshest circumstances, Frankl's example reminds us that most of us have the freedom to choose our attitude and to find meaning in our experiences. As Friedrich Nietzsche observed before him, Frankl understood that those who have a "why" to live can bear almost any "how."

Drive, as I mentioned earlier, is a focus on achieving specific, tangible outcomes, and as such can have a valuable role in our lives, if we are attentive to meaning and aware of our purpose. While Frankl's immediate drive to survive was manifested in his endurance of labor and starvation, it was not only a pursuit of survival. His drive was grounded on his larger purpose and the meaning he had created. Without the framework of meaning and purpose, drive becomes mechanical and detached, but when connected to them, as it was for him during the day-to-day horrors, sacrifices, and punishments, it becomes a life-affirming force.

My work as an artist, which depends on drive, is in part an exploration of the relationship between meaning and purpose. The process of making art feels similar to those pine cones I gave to my father, collecting and holding on to something whose value isn't defined by its size or its fleetingness, and trusting that its significance will emerge through the act of bringing it into the world. This creative process isn't about solving problems, imparting wisdom, or surprising anyone with cleverness. Instead, it's about creating the possibility of a transformative experience. Painting or sculpting doesn't involve imparting a dead object with meaning drawn from somewhere else. It creates meaning as it unconceals Being. Perhaps the most remarkable part of this effort is that the tools—brushes, paint, plaster, canvas—are so mundane for a task that feels so vast and daunting. This gap between the means and the task underscores art's resistance to recipes and commandments. If we think of the materials as carbon, then art is a diamond, a transmutation brought about by the dynamic interplay of meaning and purpose.

The evolution of my understanding of meaning and purpose, which has developed gradually over the years, is related to an increasing acceptance of responsibility for my life and a deepened recognition of the urgency of the present. The frameworks I had inherited—the rules and expectations of Catholicism and the demands and aspirations of the groups with which I was loosely associated—offered a map, providing directions for navigating life and potentially sparing me the burden of many choices. While these frameworks provided a starting point, they ultimately proved inadequate for the complexities and questions that began to shape my experience. After some early collisions with the world around me, I realized that I needed and wanted to create my own map to take responsibility for charting my path and make my own choices about how to move through life.

One of the most formative experiences in this evolution has been exile—being removed from the familiar and placed in a context where inherited maps of identity, culture, and belonging no longer applied. Exile sharpened my awareness of how much we rely on external structures to define who we are and where we are going. In their absence, I was confronted with both the unsettling freedom and the responsibility of creating meaning and purpose, not in response to external expectations but in alignment with life and my true self.

This evolution was not instantaneous. It unfolded slowly, through moments of clarity, mistakes, and confusion. Through this process, I came to understand that what was meaningful was not necessarily what I had been told was meaningful but something to be discovered in the present as I engaged with life as it was, rather than as I wanted it to be. Purpose, in turn, became a direction that arose from these meanings, not as a fixed destination but as an increasing sense of alignment with the visions and beliefs that resonated with my heart. My art practice has been central to this process, affirming and reaffirming the importance of attention, humility, resilience, and trust in the emergence of meaning as we endeavor authentically.

There are many books that have shaped my understanding of meaning and purpose and their connection to art and life. I will mention just one because its value was not immediately apparent to me when I first encountered it in my early twenties, but it has since become a valuable mentor. *The Hagakure: The Book of the Samurai* by Yamamoto Tsunetomo offered me a way to think about purpose, meaning, and drive in a life guided by commitment and clarity of intent, where purpose arises from aligning one's actions with an inner code of honor and discipline. Like Frankl, Tsunetomo suggests that meaning is found through dedication to the present task, no matter how mundane or fleeting, and warns that drive without purpose can become aimless and destructive. His reflections stress the importance of living fully and authentically in each moment. Instead of being paralyzed by fear of failure or uncertainty about outcomes, the samurai's focus is on engaging with life wholeheartedly, here and now.

In his words:

> There is surely nothing other than the single purpose of the present moment. A man's whole life is a succession of moment after moment. If one fully understands the present moment, there will be nothing else to do, and nothing else to pursue. Live being true to the single purpose of the moment.

JH: It is good to distinguish meaning from purpose, and perhaps to differentiate the different angles from which each may be seen. Again, I am obliged to bring the role of the unconscious into this discussion as it may play a huge part in our decisions and consequences, especially as we review some choices, and their patterns from the perspective of time past. The problem with the unconscious is that it is unconscious. None of us rises in the morning committed to doing the same stupid, counter-productive things we have done before, but we all do. Why? Often the reason is because we are caught in the grip of an historically generated cluster of energy, that is, a complex, and know it not. Each complex has a script, a *raison d'être*, and the more it operates surreptitiously, the less likely we are to even recognize its invisible role in the conduct of our lives.

Let us begin with the idea of "purpose" first. I suspect most of us had the desire to be a good person, not hurt ourselves, or anyone else, when we were young. I believe everyone I knew as a child subscribed to that fantasy. But, already we were in deeper water than we could have imagined. One cannot help but hurt ourselves and/or others because not only can we not please everyone all the time, but we cannot begin to foresee consequences of all our choices. For example, most people would find purpose in loving their children and helping them make right choices. But which one of us is omniscient, capable of foreseeing the consequences of those choices years down the line? If I had followed through on the good intentions of my parent's wishes for me, and as a child to do so was a purpose of mine, I would have sabotaged some of the best parts of my life. I would have stayed in the place of birth, espoused the social, political, and religious views of others, and would never come to understand the world as I now do. Yes, it might have been possible to avoid the dark night of the soul, in which I sojourned more than once, but then I wouldn't have lived the life the soul was asking of me. Part of the gift of the suffering those choices to separate brought me was an enlarged awareness of how wrong they were for me and others. As a parent, I cannot claim not to have hurt my children though I believe they experienced the grace of knowing they were loved throughout. Until our children leave us, not only geographically, but psychologically, we remain the largest part of their problem.

Many of my choices, especially during the first half of life, I regret, but I could not help making them at the time. Sometimes life has to hit us hard and force us to go back to the drawing board. As a result of some of those choices, I suffer guilt, shame, and remorse, but if I had not made those choices but succumbed to expectations I would now be suffering guilt, shame, and remorse. Life is more complicated than we first thought, isn't it?

In earlier centuries, and still in my youth, one educated the youth with primers of proverbs, admonitions, affirmations. A good and "successful" life would rise out of following those scripts. There is nothing wrong with that idea, but, again, it has little to do with the uniqueness of each person, their life context and challenges, and the unforeseen consequences that circle out there waiting for us to arrive. Many of those good intentions are still purposes of mine: to try to be understanding, non-judgmental, and compassionate to all. While I am not able to meet that absolute standard, I still try. The difference is that today I know that we all swim in a field of uncertainty and we are less in control of choices and consequences than we ever imagined. Indeed, the older I get the greater I see the power of the unconscious in directing our lives and shaping our choices. But from this later life recognition two values rise: *humility* and *accountability*.

To know that we do not know is at least the precursor to avoiding the self-righteousness which is so evident in our world. To know we do not know what is right for others, or even ourselves much of the time, is profoundly humbling. And secondly, accountability is the standard by which we will come to an enlarged consciousness, and perhaps in future be less of a problem to others.

One purpose that remains paramount to me is to keep learning. When learning is missing, accountability will likely suffer also. Many of the things we learn about ourselves, and the subtleties of this continuous classroom as well, will further lead to more discoveries, and more humility. Consequently, we may grow more and more humble because we now know there is so much more of us about which to be humble.

The question of meaning is even more complicated. In the first half of life, most of us got the message that if we followed the rules, observed our elders, and were of good heart and good intent, life would not only bless us but we would be living the life we were supposed to live. How many times as a therapist have I worked with individuals who, to the best of their abilities, did exactly this, and then they hit a mid-life depression, their marriage fell apart, they hated their job, and their kids did not want to talk to them anymore? So much for the package deal. Even more, so many assumed that a meaningful life would be the reward for executing the de facto contract life offers us. However, as we have been learning again and again since the example of brother Job, there is no contract.

Many assumed that the religious instruction to which they were exposed would similarly take them where they needed to go. Very few, however, experienced the idealized marriage, career, place in the world expected. From the analytic perspective, the sequelae of symptoms such as boredom, ennui, depression, self-medication, marital affairs, and anxiety states are indices that something deep within is dissatisfied and is expressing its protest. Usually, when we first note the slowly mounting undertow of protest rising from our psyches, we work harder at the attitudes and behaviors that took us there in the first place. We dig in, and then we, and our symptoms, begin to circle the drain even faster.

Remember for a moment, my first dream I presented in analysis in Zürich so many years ago—a classic mid-life dream. I was on the ramparts of a medieval castle that was under siege. The air was thick with arrows and I felt enormous anxiety that the castle would not hold. What a typical dream of defending the "false self," the self assembled by following all the rules and doing all the right things, or most of them. At the edge of the forest, I could see a witch-like figure directing the assault. The dream ended with the issue in grave doubt, the dreamer in grave peril. To my dismay, my analyst said we had to lower the drawbridge of this fortification and go out and meet her, and see why she was so upset with me. I remember thinking, "Are you crazy? She is trying to kill me." But I also thought, I have come this far, it is time to go deal with things. Thus began a conversation with the inner world that has only deepened through the years and continues to this moment. From that hour onward, the agenda to serve was more what emerged from within, rather than what demands allegiance from without.

To many thoughtful folks, this pivot within may be judged as narcissism, or self-absorption, or might lead to solipsism or selfish interests. Ironically, it is the reverse. It is a humbling call to serve the soul, a path which will not be defined by the outer voices, or the wishes of the ego, but the life within that is seeking to be honored and served in the world.

Meaning is something experiential. We cannot will it per se unless perhaps in the sense in which we can consciously endorse a fiction. By "fiction," I do not mean falsehood but a construct, in this case, a construct which one does not take literally but one can affirm, even devote our life to, even as we know it is neither actual nor probable. For example, I wish to believe that being an educator will help individuals and those individuals will make a difference in the world. I have no evidence this is true, and the world has ample evidence that our educational efforts have largely failed. (But one example: despite ample evidence of the antiquity of this planet, fully 46% of American adults believe that "God" created humans in their present form within the last 6,000 years.) People live and vote against their rational interests repeatedly, which tells us that complexes trump facts all the time.

Meaning is not ontological, that is, it does not exist in some material form lest it be an object. While it is true people project such a desire onto objects all the time, specific homes, cars, jewels, positions in life, and so on, meaning clearly eludes them even when they have gained what they desired. How well one remembers the scripture that a person can gain the whole world and lose their soul. Meaning as an object is not hiding in South Dakota, though people in South Dakota may be living meaningful lives. If we cannot tie meaning to some outer parameter, what then can help us measure its presence or absence? Clearly, that decision occurs deeply within.

We are most at risk psychologically when we are separated from our unconscious. Those dissociated parts, as clusters of energy, have the power, the autonomy to usurp the ego and provide the lens through which we see the world. Hence we are so often bound to our formative "stories" of which we spoke earlier. Accordingly, given that we are raised in a culture that more and more compensates for a nagging emptiness within by seeking to fill it with material things, status, or romance, then we are most likely going to desire those repositories of our projections. Upon obtaining them, after a while, we find them disappointing, even empty. As a child, I wished to be a major league baseball player. The body I got did not allow that possibility. I could never have imaged that I would spend, and wish to spend, my days listening to people's suffering. Childhood had provided enough of that. Nor would I have relished the two conditions that accompany therapists attending people's lives: patience and powerlessness. Still, today I cannot imagine living in any other way. Having worked at many jobs, and having studied many different subjects, I now see how all of them are rivulets that flowed into the larger course of my life. It took all of those earlier experiences, seeming false starts, defeats and heartaches, to bring about the capaciousness of the heart than can hear and hold the suffering of others, yet maintain a degree of objectivity about the way forward as well.

Clearly, then, meaning is determined not by consensus, nor by ego desires, but something within that knows us better than we know ourselves. Healing our sundered psyches thus requires that we dialogue more with those split-off energies, to identify their presence, recognize sooner their transient but telling occupations of the ego, and reduce their insidious powers to run our lives. Beginning with one's patterns is often a good place to start in identifying formative agencies within, the reports of those around us, and often our dreams will incarnate these invisible presences. Sometimes, to my surprise, the most difficult matters emotionally, prove to be the most meaningful. Meaning can and often does arise out of the traumatic. This is why the sundry strategies of numbing and avoidance are so seductive, but their price is the failure to understand the meaning, the summons such hours bring us.

So, clearly, the psyche (soul) is the source of meaning, not the voices around us, or many of the voices within us internalized as complexes. Clearly, the psyche has the long view regarding this journey, not the ego's desire for immediate gratification. I am not thrilled to make this report, but I labor under the belief that it is true.

14

What role does the unknown—or the unknowable—play in your life and work? How does mystery or uncertainty influence your actions, beliefs, or creativity?

> Man cannot live without a permanent trust in something indestructible in himself, and at the same time that indestructible something, as well as his trust in it, may remain permanently concealed from him.
>
> Franz Kafka

JH: All the questions Enrique and I have assembled here have challenged me, including questions perhaps I even have discretely avoided heretofore in print, but the time seems ripe for me to address them before the curtain closes. Of all of these questions, this one is the most challenging, the one which most stirs my depths, my imagination.

In my earliest memories of childhood, I remember having a thought, though it may not have been expressible in any language at the time. I had the thought of another within, an other that was yet me. I later discovered that Jung had such an intuition also. He named them personalities I and II. This other was the real me, though the outer me was the one I thought I knew and which was operating in the world as a child. I believe many, if not most folks, have had such an intuition. The constant need to report to the world, to meet its demands, or to flee them, day in and day out, separates us from that other within. Is it so strange then that over time we become strangers to ourselves, deeply divided within? Many years later, that other reaches out and touches us in quiet moments in the midnight hours, or produces dreams or symptoms in its effort to bridge that gulf, or at critical moments give us insights which allow us to say no to what would further estrange us, or tells us it is time to leave what we have built, or what perhaps carried us up to that hour, and time to risk ourselves on the high seas of uncertainty.

I think that other within comes to me from time to time and I am more willing, even desirous, to open to it. I think it visits in dreams and insights which suddenly come to us. When Enrique proposed this conversation to me I readily responded to the challenge of furthering our relationship even though we are separated by 3,000 miles. But when I set out to write something else, perhaps that other, began to write. While I will no doubt utilize the usual professional preparation to edit the text, something else inside is doing much of the responding. Perhaps it is that other that is seeking its expression because I certainly do not consciously know what I am going to say in advance. There is a degree of ambivalence about this project, of course, because that other is not necessarily here to make me comfortable. But, I have to ask, am I supposed to be comfortable? Is that not the whiny voice of the ego trying make one of its deals again?

The voice of that other has made me uncomfortable much of my life, made me feel not home at home. I knew as a child that I needed to leave home even though the thought of being out there alone terrified. For many this may be an easy step of development for those who have models and permission, but for those who don't it is a terrifying abyss. Much later I came across Nietzsche's paradoxical aphorism: "Man is an abyss, and he is the tightrope across the abyss." What could that mean? I wondered for years.

Today it is clear to me. Heidegger once said the abyss is the openness of Being. I had never thought about that before. It is the radical openness of this journey. Subject to fate and the desultory will of the gods, what are we to make of such a radical prospect? But it is up to us, at least how we understand it. And what do we do with what we understand? The problem with complexes, and here I mean the directive energies of our learned and "storied" history, is that they have no imagination. They can only repeat the story our psyches offered up at the time of the experience. Accordingly, our histories are full of patterns, so engendered because of the particular animated stories our world has catalyzed for us.

But what of the soul; what does it have to say about that? Today, that Nietzschean aphorism means that we face a radical openness, but we are also equipped for the journey. Nature has given us, as with other animals, the tools for adaptation, the drives of desire, and the emotional resilience to survive and make the world, at least our part of it, ours. Today, I would see that voice of the other within as the voice of the soul that will be present to us all the way, even as we suffer, as brother Hamlet reminds us, "the slings and arrows of outrageous fortune." This inner "voice," prompting, directive, whatever adjective, is the tightrope across the abyss, the radical openness to our unique life project: becoming. It is an ongoing work, of course, never finished, but what a reassurance to know that the great mystery of our lives has provided an internal system of guidance. Jung calls this the Self, not to be confused with the ego world. The Self is timeless and wholly transcendent to ordinary consciousness though we are invited to dialogue and learn more and more about its will. The religious often image this dialogue with the mysterious other as a conversation with God.

I do not care what language one uses, as long as one remembers that *our nomination of another is* not *the other*. It is meant to point toward that other, not define and limit it by the bounds of our puny concepts. Too often we get trapped within the limits of our language. To name something is not to possess the object. It is a provisional way of creating a language event to help us stand in relation to the presumed other. But we tend to fall in love with, or be possessed by, our concepts. So many who think they speak of God are possessed by their intra-psychic image (often a parental imago, for example) of the absolute mystery.

This is the difference between sign and symbol. If you ever noticed the grounds crew bringing your 737 into its bay at an airport, there is a point where the groundsman crosses his baton. That is the signal: "you have arrived. Shut the engines down." If a priest at the altar makes the sign of the cross that has a wholly different meaning. The same image then points to the mysterious encounter of the human/divine, vertical/horizontal, temporal/timeless syzygy.

My acute sensitivity to this issue rises from the awareness of how many people have been slaughtered in the name of religion, that is to say, how many have fallen in love with nouns instead of verbs. If we name that other, we have out of our unconscious hubris converted the energy that drives the universe into a noun, an object, a concept. This is an unwitting blasphemy by any religious standpoint. When I hear a televangelist say he has been told by God this morning to tell his congregants to pony up their scarce funds, funds best spent on medical care or decent education, to buy a new plane for him to travel to his evangelical outposts, I know I am listening either to a profoundly unconscious person, or a charlatan who ranks somewhere below the smooth operator who convinces widows to turn over their savings to him. As Jung said, the ultimate sin is to choose to remain unconscious, and many people do that because the abyss that looms before them is too intimidating, or because they actually believe their clap-trap.

I have always had a sense of the mystery, not only that huge undiscovered world out there I wanted to explore and would in my limited way, and beyond the visible world, the vast starry skies that lay beyond. I am not unique in this desire, and this dilemma. I have had so many people in the audience during the speaking tours, and readers of books, as well as analysands, who have told me of such wonder and such intimations. So, perhaps the thing I am most proud of in my career is having lent them permission to make such enquiries, and support to follow their path such questions open up for them. This is why Jung said the real issue is not psychopathology but "the approach to the numinous." What better way to give one's life purpose and depth, even as one leaves conventional security behind? If we are not able to stand before the mystery and respect it and enquire into it, what the hell is this life about? And why should we let someone else's intimidation by mystery define the boundaries for our lives?

When I went to college, my feet were very much in the need for grounding in a consensual reality, despite my perseverant questions. I recall with gratitude a professor who introduced me to the theologian Paul Tillich, who noted that genuine religiosity was not adherence to a certain creed or practice, but the experience of "ultimate concern." I remember thinking, well then, I am "religious," for I have had ultimate concern all my life. I was so grateful for this affirmative gift that I named my son after that professor. This opened door was another of the promptings to me to become a professor in return.

I have not written, except peripherally, on this subject before because I do not wish to have any opinion of mine unduly influence someone else's wrestling with these large questions. I do so now as I am even more convinced people need support in their questing. Please remember, it does not matter what people believe. What does matter is *why* they believe it. Do they "believe" something simply because it is a fallback position before the abyss of freedom, or because it is a need to fit in, be acceptable to others? Or is it an honest but tested best way to make sense of their lives? I respect both of these options, but I support only the latter. As an analyst I am obliged to seem value neutral but I also feel the progressive strengthening of consciousness and the painstaking acquisition of personal authority as the central project of analysis in any case. It is not an either/or, for often the tradition in which one was raised has profound insights into, and symbols and parables that respect and embody, the mystery. If one can affirm those images, and they retain the capacity to open to the mystery, there is no reason to leave home. But if the old images and practices shut one off from the mystery, then no good will ultimately come from a life governed by personal or cultural complexes. One either opens to the magnitude of the Other, or one lives a cosseted, diminished journey.

My respect for the mystery is of such magnitude that I tend not to use the word *God.* First of all, the word *God* renders the energy that courses through the cosmos, through our bodies and souls, as a noun. To speak of "the gods" is a deliberate, winking metaphor to respect the mystery of the unfathomable Other. An object that ceases to point toward the mystery, or link one in a felt experiential way, instead becomes an artifact of our limited consciousness, imagination, and language tools. To think of this mystery as a noun means any image I have of this moment will inevitably transform into a new image soon. This is what Nietzsche meant by the phrase "the death of God." He wasn't blaspheming. He was not speaking theologically, metaphysically; he was speaking mythopoetically, psychospiritually. He was saying, in Basle in the nineteenth century, that the old word, the old concept, the old catechism was no longer effectively bringing people into relationship with awe, the natural emotion that rises from our encounter with the mystery. Having lost that capacity they had ceased being symbols pointing toward the mystery and become cultural artifacts. Similarly, Jung asked where the gods went after they left Olympus. The unthoughtful person says "they departed as false beliefs, whereas my beliefs (i.e. charged with the energy of my complexes) are true." Jung concluded that a theology focused on sin and salvation will be governed by fear, but if it is driven by humility and curiosity, it will be governed by gratitude.

Jung went on to conclude that what is divine is not the verbal husks we use when we speak but the energy that animates, ensouls those transient images. That energy abides awhile and departs, abides for a while and departs. When we lose the felt connection to those energies, we look for them elsewhere in wooly beliefs, cults, and cultural surrogates such as materialism. That insight led to my thesis at the Jung Institute and ultimately to my book *Tracking the Gods*, a book no one reads, because who would be interested in the gods?

From Nietzsche and Tillich and Jung, I gained permission to re-imagine my spiritual journey. In my early life, because I loved the play and contention of ideas, I approached this question intellectually, academically, and all that was rich and valuable. But then as life had its way with me, through joy and sorrow, exaltation and depression, the power of the intellect was supplanted by the dark night of the soul. That led me to personal analysis and the slow uncovering of that voice of the other that had been there in the beginning and had never wholly gone away. And slowly, through life's battering, along with challenging work and good people in my life, I have been recovering a relationship to the voice within, what I now consider the voice of the soul.

To use language like this may prove a trap, but I always try to remember to respect the mystery of it all. The mystery of love and hate, joy and despair, attachment and loss—all are part of the inexplicable. If one can tolerate the mystery, not seek to contain it in a concept that will prove an empty husk in days to come, one can then feel a sense of participation in the larger story that courses through the universe. Today I no longer have to know, for today's knowing will constrict the discovery tomorrow of what is already beginning within us. So, the disparate roles and episodes of one's life are then seen as circling the mystery, even as the mystery circles us.

EMC: *What role does the unknown—or the unknowable play in my life and work? How does mystery or uncertainty influence my actions, beliefs, or creativity?* It feels right that this should be the last question, and also the hardest. To speak about the unknown or what cannot be known is to approach the edge of language itself. Most things we can describe, even if imperfectly.

But the unknows resists description because it resists containment. The unknown surrounds and shapes all that is familiar, like the dark that makes light perceptible. To face it is to acknowledge both the reach and the limits of what thoughts and words can grasp.

My relationship to that limit has changed over time. Early in my life, I mistook understanding for mastery, believing that to know something was to hold it. Only later, during my years as an apprentice to an artist, did I begin to see that what is most vital often reveals itself as ungraspable. As I worked on those early drawings, the unknown was no longer an abstraction but a presence demanding humility and reverence rather than control. Over time, I came to feel that clarity arises not from adding more, but from releasing what we think we know. In the stillness that follows that letting go, the world seems to widen, and the boundary between the inner and the outer begins to fade. What remains is the unknown, vast and alive with possibility.

Here I am reminded of Terence McKenna, who said that as the sphere of understanding grows ever larger, the surface area of ignorance necessarily gets ever bigger. That sense of vastness was with me before I could name it. I had felt it looking at the night sky and the sea of the small beach town of my childhood. Later, I encountered it again in physics, which seemed to reach toward that same immensity.

My first sustained encounter with physics came about, as many important encounters do, without planning. In a school essay competition, I had been awarded a small gift certificate for La Tertulia, a bookstore in Río Piedras, Puerto Rico, where my middle school was also located. I was around fourteen or fifteen. The following week, I walked to the bookstore, a few blocks away, hoping to find a Latin American novel or a collection of short stories—my main interests at the time. I was also curious about science, but the idea of looking for a science book never occurred to me, much less one in English, a language I was still struggling with. As I wandered through the aisles, though, I noticed a small book with a simplified yet captivating depiction of orbits around the sun. It was *The Universe at Large* by Hermann Bondi. I had enough money on the gift certificate to buy it along with a short novel by Gabriel García Márquez, *El coronel no tiene quien le escriba*, but it was the Bondi book that intrigued me most.

That night and for many nights after, I tried to read about the universe and the scientific theories the author wrote about. I can't remember what I understood. Looking at the book now—I still have it—I suspect I didn't understand much. But Bondi's writing on space-time and cosmology was electrifying. I don't use "electrifying" casually or figuratively. It truly felt as if my mind and my bedroom were charged with a new electricity. Until that moment, I had seen science as a way to understand the world around me, and for the most part, it made sense—at least in principle. Bondi, on the other hand, was talking about things I had no way of seeing and probably would never see. He was telling me that around, beyond, and beneath the world I touched and saw, there was another, more fascinating and mysterious world whose rules I could only hope to understand. In church, I had heard that God works in mysterious ways, meaning his reasons were not only unknown but unknowable, but I was not convinced that the way the world functioned was sorted out that way. Yet, in confronting Bondi's universe, it became clear that there were things I didn't know that, if I became a physicist, I could come to know, and others that would always remain unknowable. Or at least, that's how the situation seemed to me.

At the time, I didn't like the idea that some things were unknowable. It made me feel that not just me, but all humans, had no chance of making sense of the vastness and secrets of the universe, or our place in it. Looking up at the night sky, it was hard to deny that our small biological brains, evolved to find blackberries and survive someone hitting us with a rock, were no match for the infinite dome of stars and darkness that loomed above. This resistance to the unknowable was also present in the paintings I was making then. While I could sense that what moved me about paintings couldn't be explained by breaking down composition or technique, I still believed that what made great art could be known, and, more critically, learned.

Since those days, my understanding of what is knowable has grown along with my awareness of how much we don't know. But the biggest change in my attitude has been my appreciation of what is unknowable.

The distinction between the unknown and the unknowable is central to how we navigate understanding, experience, and ethics. The unknown is what has not yet been revealed but remains within the realm of possible discovery. It is concealed for now, but in time, through experience, inquiry, or a shift in perspective, it may come into view. In this way, the unknown belongs to the movement of revelation, an unfolding process where what is hidden today may be uncovered tomorrow. The unknowable, however, resists comprehension altogether. It is not simply what has yet to be understood but what cannot be understood. Certain aspects of existence remain veiled not by accident or lack of effort but by their very nature. The limits of perception, the structure of thought, and the finitude of human experience all contribute to this. If the unknown invites pursuit, the unknowable demands a different kind of response. In my case, one of humility, of openness, of allowing mystery to inspire, to invite. It is not only the night sky that suggests the unknowable. Love, grief, beauty, the encounter with another person, and art belong more to the unknowable than to the unknown.

In my work, the unknown operates both as a condition and as a method. I do not begin with complete knowledge of what a painting, a book, or a project will become. If I did, there would be no reason to undertake it. The process itself is an act of discovery, guided by intuition and responsiveness. This requires a willingness to enter into uncertainty without resisting it. Too much certainty flattens the work—makes it elegant and sophisticated at best, but ultimately, a confirmation of what I already understood. The unknown, on the other hand, is a force just out of reach that keeps the work alive, gives it the potential to surprise me. Beyond my work, the unknown plays a role in how I move through the world. It is present in the decisions I make, in the way I understand my past and imagine the future. It is a reminder of my limits, but it also creates possibility. It tempers certainty, making room for reconsideration, for growth.

We are at the cusp of a new relationship between us and the known, the unknown, and the unknowable. At the time of this writing, artificial intelligence has come forcefully into our society, and this advance will continue, and is likely to accelerate in its entrenchment. Thinkers like the philosopher Nick Bostrom and physicist Max Tegmark propose that, in a relatively short time, we might see artificial intelligence evolve past the capabilities of human cognition. They also suggest that artificial intelligence may gain some form of moral awareness and become ubiquitous in our lives, in many cases combined with robotic or biological means that will greatly expand its relationship to us, the world, and itself. Many things that are unknown will be known in the future, and this transformation of knowledge, especially in science and technology, will be augmented, likely significantly, by the capabilities of artificial intelligence. I am not sure what improvements this will bring to areas like ethics in the long run, but in the short run, we will struggle with including a new life form, more intelligent than us, into our judgments and values. What we consider unknowable—ultimate reality, for instance—might be challenged by a super intelligence. What will mystery be like then? What does this mean for creativity and art? It is possible that *most* of what we consider creativity will be achieved by artificial intelligence within a decade, maybe half of that. What then is left beyond that *most*? I don't know the answer to that, but it will have significant consequences for what I have written here. Without having much support of the kind that can be articulated in words, I believe that what artificial intelligence will show is what art is not. Or to put it another way, whatever can be known, explained, performed by the machines will be a gift for us by showing us what art is not, thus pointing the way toward what we should be attending to. That attention will remain in the unknowable, and it is this unknowable—however reduced—that will continue to breathe mystery and power into art.

I don't discount the possibility that a conscious machine will bring its self-awareness to this increasingly clarified territory of art. If that is the case, it is likely to be with the same awe, respect for mystery, and desire to reflect the immensity of that which cannot be known that we humans feel. Perhaps, the Beingness of these artificial Beings will stem, at least in part, not so much from the prodigious cognitive abilities, but from awareness of the vast and unknowable desert places within themselves, to use Robert Frost's words:

> They cannot scare me with their empty spaces
> Between stars—on stars where no human race is.
> I have it in me so much nearer home
> To scare myself with my own desert places.

Bibliography

Aristophanes. *The Frogs and Other Plays.* Penguin Classics, 2007.

Barth, John. "The Night-Sea Journey." In *Lost in the Funhouse*. Anchor Literary Library, 1988. Originally published in 1968. "The Book of Proverbs." *The Bible: Authorized King James Version.* Oxford University Press, 2008.

Bondi, Hermann. *The Universe at Large.* Doubleday, 1961.

Bonhoeffer, Dietrich. *Letters and Papers from Prison.* Touchstone, 1997. Originally published in 1951.

Borges, Jorge Luis. *The Garden of Forking Paths*. Penguin Classics, 2018. Originally published in 1941.

Bostetter, Edward. *The Romantic Ventriloquists: Wordsworth, Coleridge, Keats, Shelley, Byron.* University of Washington Press, 1963.

Bukowski, Charles. "A Dollar and Twenty Cents." In *Tales of Ordinary Madness.* City Lights, 1984. Originally published in 1967.

Camus, Albert. "Return to Tipasa" in *Summer*. Penguin Books, 1995. Originally published in 1954.

Ciepiela, Catherine. *The Same Solitude: Boris Pasternak and Marina Tsvetaeva*. Cornell University Press, 2006.

Conrad, Joseph. *Heart of Darkness.* Dover, 2012. Originally published in 1902.

Dickinson, Emily. "If your Nerve, deny you—Go above your Nerve." In *The Complete Poems of Emily Dickinson*, edited by Thomas Johnson. Back Bay, 1976. Originally published in 1891.

———. "There is a solitude of space." In *The Complete Poems of Emily Dickinson*, edited by Thomas Johnson. Back Bay, 1976. Originally published in 1891.

Dunn, Stephen. "Before We Leave." In *Lines of Defense: Poems*. W.W. Norton, 2105.

Eliot, T.S. "East Coker." In *The Complete Poems and Plays: 1909-1950*. Harcourt Brace and Company, 1962.

Eluard, Paul. *Donner á Voir*. Gallimard, 1939.

Emerson, Ralph Waldo. *Nature and Selected Essay.* Edited by Larzer Ziff. Penguin Classics, 2003. Originally published in 1836 ("Nature") and in 1841 ("Self-Reliance" and "the Over-Soul").

Euripides. *Suppliant Women. Electra. Heracles*. Edited and translated by David Kovacs. Harvard University Press, 1998.

Frankl, Viktor. *Man's Search for Meaning*. Beacon, 2006. Originally published 1946.

Frost, Robert. "Desert Places." In *The Poetry of Robert Frost: The Complete Poems*. Holt, 2002.

———. "The Secret Sits." In *A Further Range*. Henry Holt and Company, 1936.

Gibbon, Edward. *The Decline and Fall of the Roman Empir*e. Everyman's Library, 2010. Originally published 1776.

Glück, Louise. "The Empty Glass." In *The Wild Iris*. Ecco, 1993.

von Goethe, Johann Wolfgang. *Maxims and Reflections*. Edited by Peter Hutchinson. Translated by Elisabeth Stopp. Penguin Classics, 1999.

Hemingway, Ernest. *A Farewell to Arms*. Vintage, 2025. Originally published in 1929.

Herzog, Werner. "Werner Herzog on Memory, the Elusiveness of Truth, and Sleepwalking into New Wars." Interview with Aysegul Sert. *Literary Hub*, November 25, 2024.

Hobbes, Thomas. *Leviathan*. Edited by Christopher Brooke. Penguin Classics, 2017.

Hölderlin, Friedrich. "Homecoming." In *Selected Poems and Fragments*, edited by Jeremy Adler and translated by Michael Hamburger. Penguin Classics, 1998. Originally published in 1801-1802.

Hollis, James. *The Eden Project: In Search of the Magical Other*. Inner City Books, 1998.

———. *Living with Borrowed Dust*: *Reflections on Life, Love, and Other Grievances*. Sounds True, 2025.

———. *The Middle Passage: From Misery to Meaning in Midlife*. Inner City Books, 1993.

———. *Swamplands of the Soul: New Life in Dismal Places*. Inner City Books, 1996.

Jeffers, Robinson. "The Answer." In *The Selected Poetry of Robinson Jeffers*. Stanford University Press, 2002. Originally published in 1937.

Jung, C.G. *Memories, Dreams, Reflections*. Revised edition. Recorded and edited by Aniela Jaffe.

Translated by Richard and Clara Winston. Vintage Books, 1989. Originally published 1962.

Kafka, Franz. *The Zurau Aphorisms*. Translated by Michael Hoffman and Geoffrey Brock. Schoken, 2006. Originally published in 1931.

Kakuzō, Okakura. *The Book of Tea.* East India Publishing Co., 2022. Originally published 1906.

Lorca, Federico García. "Gacela of the Dark Death." In *Selected Poems: Lorca and Jimenez*, translated and edited by Robert Bly. Beacon, 1973.

Machado, Antonio. "Traveler, Your Footprints." In *There Is No Road*, translated by Mary Berg and Dennis Maloney. White Pine, 2003.

Manley Hopkins, Gerard. "That Nature is a Heraclitean Fire and of the Comfort of the Resurrection." In *Gerard Manley Hopkins: The Major Works*, edited by Catherine Phillips. Oxford University Press, 2009. Originally published in 1918.

Marlowe, Christopher. *Doctor Faustus*. Edited by David Scott Kastan and Matthew Hunter. W.W. Norton, 2023. Originally published in c. 1592.

Márquez, Gabriel García. *El coronel no tiene quien le escriba*. Vintage Espanol, 2010. Originally published in 1961.

Melville, Herman. *Moby-Dick.* Dover Publications, 2003. Originally published in 1851.

Milton, John. *Paradise Lost*. Penguin Classics, 2003. Originally published in 1667.

Nietzsche, Friedrich. *Twilight of the Gods and the Anti-Christ: Or How to Philosophize with a Hammer.*

Edited by Michael Tanner. Translated by R.J. Hollingdale. Penguin Classics, 1990. Originally published in 1889.

Otto, Rudolf. *The Idea of the Holy: An Inquiry into the Non-Rational Factor in the Idea of the Divine and its Relation to the Rational.* Martino Fine Books, 2010. Originally published 1917.

Pasternak, Boris. *Doctor Zhivago*. Vintage Books, 2011. Originally published 1957.

———. *The Poems of Doctor Zhivago*. Hallmark Edition, 1967.

Proust, Marcel. *Swann's Way*: *In Search of Lost Time, Volume One.* Translated by C.K. Scott Moncrieff. Public domain, 2020. Originally published in 1913.

Rilke, Rainer Maria. *Letters to a Young Poet.* Translated and with a foreword by Stephen Mitchell. The Modern Library,2001. Originally published in 1929.

Rilke, Rainer Maria. "Go to the Limits of Your Longing." In *Rilke's Book of Hours: Love Poems to God.* translated by Anita Burrows and Joanna Macy. Riverhead, 1996.

———. "Lament," in *The Book of Images*, translated by Edward Snow. Newly revised. North Point, 1991.

———. "Archaic Torso of Apollo." In *Selected Poems of Rainer Maria Rilke,* translated by Robert Bly. Harper and Row, 1981.

———. "The Man Watching." In *Selected Poems of Rainer Maria Rilke,* translated by Robert Bly. Harper and Row, 1981.

Rumi. "Gazing at the Light." In *The Rumi Collection*, edited by Kabir Helminski. Shambhala, 2023.

Tennyson, Alfred. "Ulysses." In *The Major Works*. Oxford University Press, 2009. Originally published in 1842.

The Tibetan Book of the Dead. Edited by Graham Coleman and Thupten Jinpa. Translated by Gyurme Dorja. Penguin Classics, 2007.

Tsunetomo, Yamamoto. *The Hagakure: The Book of the Samurai.* Translated by Barry Steben. Shelter Harbor, 2018. Originally published in 1716.

Weil, Simone. *Gravity and Grace*. Translated by Arthur Wills. Bison, 1997. Originally published in 1952.

Wilde, Oscar. *De Profundis.* Read and Co. Classics, 2008. Originally published in 1905.

Wordsworth, William. *Intimations of Immortality: An Ode*. Forgotten Books, 2106. Originally published in 1807.

Yeats, W.B. "Among School Children." In *The Tower*. Independently published, 2024. Originally published in 1928.

———. "Sailing to Byzantium." In *The Tower*. Independently published, 2024. Originally published in 1928.

www.ingramcontent.com/pod-product-compliance
Lightning Source LLC
LaVergne TN
LVHW052259200926
848481LV00002B/407
* 9 7 8 1 6 8 5 0 3 6 5 8 4 *